OUT & ABOUT

An Interactive Course in Beginning English

STUDENT BOOK

Abigail Umanzor

Amy Hemmert and Rick Kappra

Alta Book Center Publishers
Post Office Box 1736
Provo, Utah 84603 USA

Tel: 800 ALTA/ESL (Mexico, Canada and USA)
Other International: 801.377.1530
Fax: 800 ALTA/FAX
International: 801.222.9199

D1219497

Acquisitions Editor: Aaron Berman
Lead Content Editor: Richard Firsten
Content and Production Editors: Jamie Ann Cross and Raissa Nina Burns
Cover Design and Interior Illustrations: Andrew Lange Illustration
Interior Design and Page Layout: Wanda Espana/Wee Design Group

Acknowledgements

We would like to thank the following people for their help in producing this book:
Aaron Berman and Simón Almendares for their leadership and vision.
Jamie Cross for her wonderful editorial insight and faultless attention to detail.
Richard Firsten for his editorial eye and sharp wit.
Raissa Nina Burns for her keen eye.
Andrew Lange for his artistic talent.
Wanda Espana for her creative design.
The many students and teachers, especially those at City College of San Francisco and Santa Cruz Adult School, who helped pilot these materials and provided us with invaluable feedback.

Dedication

*To our parents: Renold and Margaret Kappra and Bob and Nancy Lindeman
And to the memory of Laurette Lyall, who taught us how to mingle.*

Alta Book Center Publishers
Post Office Box 1736
Provo, Utah 84603 USA
Website: www.altaesl.com • Email: info@altaesl.com
Phone: 800 ALTA/ESL or 801.377.1530 (International)
Fax: 800 ALTA/FAX or 801.222.9199 (International)

ISBN: 978-1-932383-01-0
Library of Congress Control Number: 2004101328

Getting Started

Introductions

David and Jennie are classmates. They are meeting for the first time.

A: Hi, my name is David.

B: Hi, I'm Jennie.

A: Nice to meet you.

B: Nice to meet you, too.

Hi, my name is _____ .

Hi, I'm _____ .

Nice to meet you.

Nice to meet you, too.

Saying Goodbye

A: Bye, Jennie. I'll see you tomorrow.

B: Okay, David. See you.

Bye, _____ . I'll see you tomorrow.

Okay, _____ . See you.

Practice introducing yourself and saying goodbye to your classmates. Write their names.

_____

_____

_____

_____

Greetings	Goodbye
Hi.	Goodbye.
Hello.	Bye.
How are you?	See you.
	See you later.

How do you spell your name?

UNIT 1

In the Classroom

1.1 Vocabulary Presentation

1.2 Speaking

PARTNER **A:** *Look at page 3.*

PARTNER **B:** *Look at page 4. Say the words.*

PARTNER **A:** *Point to the picture.*

Change roles and repeat.

This is a book.

Open your book.

Turn to page 12.

Read page 12.

Talk to your partner.

Listen.

Repeat.

Write.

Look at the board.

 1.3 Writing

Listen to your teacher. Write the words.

1. _____   3. _____   5. _____

2. _____   4. _____   6. _____

 1.4 Complete the sentence.

1. Open your _____ .

2. Talk to your _____ .

3. Look at the _____ .

4. Read _____ 12.

5. _____ to page 12.

6. _____ is a book.

1.5 The Alphabet

A B C D E F G H I J K L M N O P Q R S T U V W X Y Z

Say and write:	*Say and write:*	*Writing Practice:*	*Writing Practice:*
A _____	a _____	A _____	a _____
B _____	b _____	B _____	b _____
C _____	c _____	C _____	c _____
D _____	d _____	D _____	d _____
E _____	e _____	E _____	e _____
F _____	f _____	F _____	f _____
G _____	g _____	G _____	g _____
H _____	h _____	H _____	h _____
I _____	i _____	I _____	i _____
J _____	j _____	J _____	j _____
K _____	k _____	K _____	k _____
L _____	l _____	L _____	l _____
M _____	m _____	M _____	m _____
N _____	n _____	N _____	n _____
O _____	o _____	O _____	o _____
P _____	p _____	P _____	p _____
Q _____	q _____	Q _____	q _____
R _____	r _____	R _____	r _____
S _____	s _____	S _____	s _____
T _____	t _____	T _____	t _____
U _____	u _____	U _____	u _____
V _____	v _____	V _____	v _____
W _____	w _____	W _____	w _____
X _____	x _____	X _____	x _____
Y _____	y _____	Y _____	y _____
Z _____	z _____	Z _____	z _____

1.6 More Classroom Vocabulary

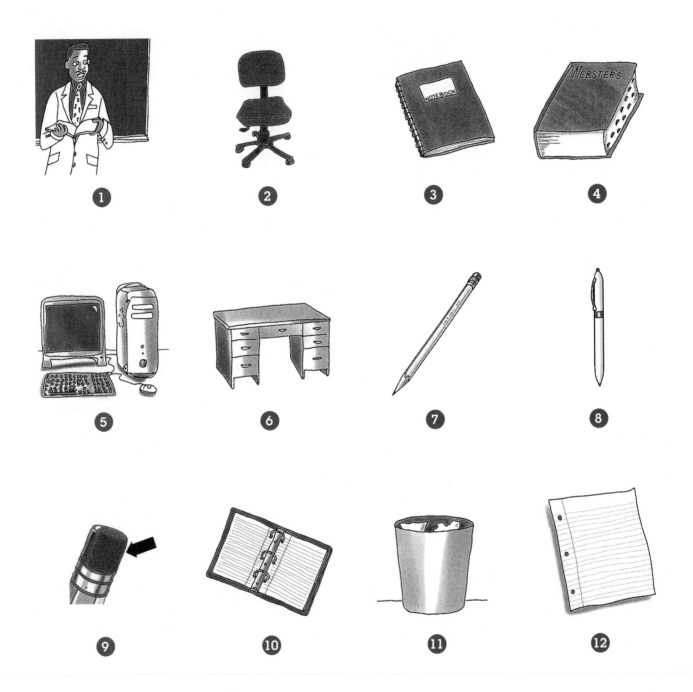

Listen and write the words.

1. _____   5. _____   9. _____

2. _____   6. _____   10. _____

3. _____   7. _____   11. _____

4. _____   8. _____   12. _____

1.7 Spelling

Work with a partner. Choose any word from the box. Spell the word to your partner. Take turns.

PARTNER **A:** computer

PARTNER **B:** How do you spell that?

PARTNER **A:** c – o – m – p – u – t – e – r

> How do you spell that?
>
> Could you repeat that, please?

Partner B writes the word on the line and gives Partner A a word to spell.

binder	chair	partner
board	calendar	pen
book	listen	pencil
clock	look	read
computer	notebook	repeat
desk	open	talk
dictionary	page	teacher
eraser	paper	wastebasket

1. _____   5. _____

2. _____   6. _____

3. _____   7. _____

4. _____   8. _____

1.8 Where is it?

| on | next to | in front of | behind |

Where is the pencil?
The pencil is **on** the book.
It's on the book.

Where is the wastebasket?
The wastebasket is **next to** the desk.
It's next to the desk.

Where is the teacher?
The teacher is **in front of** the board.
He's in front of the board.

Where is the board?
The board is **behind** the desk.
It's behind the desk.

Write a sentence for each question.

1. Where is the computer?

4. Where is the pencil?

_____

2. Where is the pencil?

5. Where is the teacher?

_____

3. Where is the pen?

6. Where is the teacher?

_____

1.9 Partner to Partner

Where's the _____?

It's _____.

on
in front of
next to
behind

Ask your partner about these things in your classroom.

pen	chair	binder	calendar
pencil	wastebasket	dictionary	clock
eraser	notebook	paper	teacher

1.10 The Numbers One to Ten

Read each number and word. Write the number. Write the word.

1 – one   _____   _____

2 – two   _____   _____

3 – three   _____   _____

4 – four   _____   _____

5 – five   _____   _____

6 – six   _____   _____

7 – seven   _____   _____

8 – eight   _____   _____

9 – nine   _____   _____

10 – ten   _____   _____

1.11   What do you have?

Do you have a pencil?   *Yes, I do.*

Do you have a pen?   *No, I don't.*

Ask your classmates about these things. Write *yes or no.*

What's your name?   **How do you spell that?**

Do you have a _____?

Name	Pencil	Pen	Binder	Notebook	Dictionary

Write about yourself. What *do you have?*

I have . . .   I don't have . . .

_____

_____

_____

_____

_____

UNIT 2

Nice to Meet You.

2.1 Vocabulary Presentation

Carlos Irizari

①

Carlos

②

Irizari

③

④

PASSPORT
PASSPORT

⑤

Ciao!

⑥

Jamie Cross
137 Evergreen Road
Youngstown, Ohio 09310

⑦

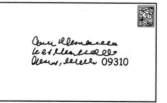

09310

⑧

973-811-0788

⑨

2.2 Speaking

PARTNER **A**: *Look at page 11.*

PARTNER **B**: *Look at page 12. Say the words.*

PARTNER **A**: *Point to the picture.*

Change roles and repeat.

What's your name?

What's your first name?

What's your last name?

Where are you from?

What's your nationality?

What language do you speak?

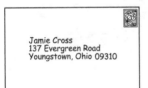

What's your address?

What's your zip code?

What's your telephone number?

2.3 Writing

Listen to your teacher. Write the words.

1. _____   3. _____   5. _____

2. _____   4. _____   6. _____

2.4 Complete the sentence.

1. My _____ is Beth.   4. My _____ is 94102.

2. I'm _____ the U.S.   5. My _____ is 202 Oak Street.

3. I _____ English.   6. My _____ is Johnson.

| 11 | 12 | 13 | 14 | 15 | 16 | 17 | 18 | 19 | 20 | 30 | 40 | 50 | 60 | 70 | 80 | 90 | 100 |

2.5 Say and Write

Listen to your teacher. Repeat the numbers. Write the numbers.

_____ _____ _____ _____ _____ _____

_____ _____ _____ _____ _____ _____

_____ _____ _____ _____ _____ _____

 ## 2.6 Partner to Partner

Say a number to your partner. Your partner will write the number. Take turns.

1. _____ 3. _____ 5. _____ 7. _____ 9. _____
2. _____ 4. _____ 6. _____ 8. _____ 10. _____

 ## 2.7 Listen and Circle

Listen and circle the number you hear.

1.   13   30   6.   12   21
2.   15   50   7.   14   40
3.   18   80   8.   17   70
4.   16   60   9.   19   90
5.   11   100   10.   13   31

 ## 2.8 Spelling

Choose a word. Spell it to your partner. Take turns.

name	first	last	native	zip	code
country	language	nationality	address	telephone	number

1. _____ 4. _____

2. _____ 5. _____

3. _____ 6. _____

2.9 More Numbers Practice

Write the number next to the word.

1. one _____   6. ten _____

2. four _____   7. three _____

3. seven _____   8. two _____

4. five _____   9. six _____

5. eight _____   10. nine _____

Write the word next to the number.

1. _____   6. _____

2. _____   7. _____

3. _____   8. _____

4. _____   9. _____

5. _____   10. _____

2.10 Talk to your classmates.

Write about yourself.

My telephone number is _____.

My address is _____.

My zip code is _____.

Ask your classmates.

What's your _____? . . . name?   . . . telephone number?   . . . address?   . . . zip code?

Name	Telephone Number	Address and Zip Code

2.11 Where are you from?

Country	Language	Nationality
Brazil	Portuguese	Brazilian
China	Chinese	Chinese
Colombia	Spanish	Colombian
Japan	Japanese	Japanese
Korea	Korean	Korean
Mexico	Spanish	Mexican
Russia	Russian	Russian
Vietnam	Vietnamese	Vietnamese
Yemen	Arabic	Yemeni

Write about yourself.

What country are you from?   I'm from _____.
What language do you speak?   I speak _____.
What's your nationality?   I'm _____.

Ask your classmates.

Name	Country	Language	Nationality

2.12 Student Information

Read the student information sheet.

Student Information

Name: _____ *Freitas* _____ *Paolo* _____
   Last   First   Middle

Address: ____ *209* _____ *Hayes Road* _____
   Number   Street   Apartment

   _____ *Seattle* _____ *Washington* _____ *98178* _____
   City   State   Zip Code

Telephone: __ *(206)   555-9604* _____   Native Country: ____ *Brazil* _____
   Area Code   Number

Native Language: __ *Portuguese* ___   Nationality: ____ *Brazilian* _____

Answer the questions.

1. What country is the student from? _____

2. What's the student's last name? _____

3. What's the student's nationality? _____

4. What's the student's middle name? _____

5. What's the student's telephone number? _____

6. What's the student's first name? _____

7. What's the student's native language? _____

8. What's the student's address? _____

2.13 Personal Information

Write about yourself.

Personal Information

Name: _____

                            Last   First   Middle

Address: _____

              Number   Street   Apartment

_____

              City   State   Zip Code

Telephone: _____   **Native Country:** _____

            Area Code   Number

Native Language: _____   **Nationality:** _____

Questions

What's your . . .?	What city do you live in?
first name	What country are you from?
last name	What language do you speak?
address	How do you spell that?
zip code	
telephone number	
nationality	

Ask your partner.

Personal Information

Name: _____

                            Last   First   Middle

Address: _____

              Number   Street   Apartment

_____

              City   State   Zip Code

Telephone: _____   **Native Country:** _____

            Area Code   Number

Native Language: _____   **Nationality:** _____

UNIT 3

What Day Is Today?

3.1 Vocabulary Presentation

January

S	M	T	W	TH	F	S
				1	2	3
4	5	6	7	8	9	10
11	12	13	14	15	16	17
18	19	20	21	22	23	24
25	26	27	28	29	30	31

❶

January

S	M	T	W	TH	F	S
				1	2	3
4	5	6	7	8	9	10
11	12	13	14	15	16	17
18	19	20	21	22	23	24
25	26	27	28	29	30	31

❷

January

S	M	T	W	TH	F	S
				1	2	3
4	5	6	7	8	9	10
11	12	13	14	15	16	17
18	19	20	21	22	23	24
25	26	27	28	29	30	31

❸

❹

82   2

❺

January

S	M	T	W	TH	F	S
				1	2	3
4	5	6	7	8	9	10
11	12	13	14	15	16	17
18	19	20	21	22	23	24
25	26	27	28	29	30	31

❻

JANUARY 2056

S	M	T	W	TH	F	S
				1	2	3
4	5	6	7	8	9	10
11	12	13	14	15	16	17
18	19	20	21	22	23	24
25	26	27	28	29	30	31

❼

❽

January

S	M	T	W	TH	F	S
				1	2	3
4	5	6	7	8	9	10
11	12	13	14	15	16	17
18	19	20	21	22	23	24
25	26	27	28	29	30	31

❾

3.2 Speaking

PARTNER **A:** *Look at page 19.*

PARTNER **B:** *Look at page 20. Say the words.*

PARTNER **A:** *Point to the picture.*

Change roles and repeat.

January						
S	M	T	W	TH	F	S
				1	2	3
4	5	6	7	8	9	10
11	12	13	14	15	16	17
18	19	20	21	22	23	24
25	26	27	28	29	30	31

What day is today?

January						
S	M	T	W	TH	F	S
				1	2	3
4	5	6	7	8	9	10
11	12	13	14	15	16	17
18	19	20	21	22	23	24
25	26	27	28	29	30	31

What is today's date?

January						
S	M	T	W	TH	F	S
				1	2	3
4	5	6	7	8	9	10
11	12	13	14	15	16	17
18	19	20	21	22	23	24
25	26	27	28	29	30	31

What month is it?

When is your birthday?

How old are you?

January						
S	M	T	W	TH	F	S
				1	2	3
4	5	6	7	8	9	10
11	12	13	14	15	16	17
18	19	20	21	22	23	24
25	26	27	28	29	30	31

What day was yesterday?

JANUARY 2056						
S	M	T	W	TH	F	S
				1	2	3
4	5	6	7	8	9	10
11	12	13	14	15	16	17
18	19	20	21	22	23	24
25	26	27	28	29	30	31

What year is it?

What time is it?

January						
S	M	T	W	TH	F	S
				1	2	3
4	5	6	7	8	9	10
11	12	13	14	15	16	17
18	19	20	21	22	23	24
25	26	27	28	29	30	31

What day is tomorrow?

3.3 Writing

Listen to your teacher. Write the words.

1. _____

2. _____

3. _____

4. _____

5. _____

6. _____

3.4 Complete the sentence.

1. What day is _____ ?

2. What is today's _____ ?

3. What _____ is it?

4. When is your _____ ?

5. How _____ are you?

6. What _____ is it?

3.5 The Days of the Week

Sunday	Monday	Tuesday	Wednesday	Thursday	Friday	Saturday

Say and spell the days of the week to your partner.

1. _____   4. _____   7. _____

2. _____   5. _____

3. _____   6. _____

What day is today?   Today is _____.

What day is tomorrow?   Tomorrow is _____.

What day was yesterday?   Yesterday was _____.

3.6 The Months of the Year

January	February	March	April	May	June
July	August	September	October	November	December

Say and spell six months of the year to your partner.

1. _____   4. _____

2. _____   5. _____

3. _____   6. _____

This month is _____. Next month is _____. Last month was _____.

Write the number next to the month.

December _____	March _____	April _____
September _____	June _____	May _____
November _____	August _____	July _____
October _____	February _____	January _____

3.7 What month is this?

Make a calendar for this month. Write the month, days of the week, and numbers.

Sunday						

What day is today?   *Today is* _____.

3.8 Ordinal Numbers

1st	2nd	3rd	4th	5th
first	second	third	fourth	fifth
6th	7th	8th	9th	10th
sixth	seventh	eighth	ninth	tenth

What is today's date?   *It is* _____.
                                                    (month)   (day)

When is your birthday? Say these dates.

My birthday is January 1st.   My birthday is February 2nd.
My birthday is March 3rd.   My birthday is April 4th.
My birthday is May 5th.   My birthday is June 6th.

Can you say these dates?

1. 7/8   4. 10/2
2. 8/6   5. 11/5
3. 9/10   6. 12/9

3.9 More Ordinal Numbers

11th	12th	13th	14th	15th
eleventh	twelfth	thirteenth	fourteenth	fifteenth
16th	17th	18th	19th	20th
sixteenth	seventeenth	eighteenth	nineteenth	twentieth

Write the numbers.

1. first   _____   6. fourteen   _____
2. two   _____   7. third   _____
3. fifth   _____   8. nine   _____
4. tenth   _____   9. twentieth   _____
5. fourth   _____   10. second   _____

3.10 Even More Ordinal Numbers

Write the numbers next to the words.

1. twenty-first   _____   7. twenty-seventh _____
2. thirtieth   _____   8. twenty-second   _____
3. twenty-fifth   _____   9. thirty-first   _____
4. twenty-eighth _____   10. twenty-ninth   _____
5. twenty-fourth _____   11. twenty-sixth   _____
6. twenty-third   _____   12. twentieth   _____

3.11 Birthday Mingle

A: When is your birthday?

B: My birthday is November 16th. When is your birthday?

A: My birthday is January 10th.

Ask your classmates about their birthdays.

Name	Birthday

3.12 Writing

Write the numbers for these dates.

1. January first   _____
2. February fourteenth   _____
3. May first   _____

4. July fourth   _____
5. October thirty-first _____
6. December twenty-fifth _____

3.13 Spelling

Partner A

Spell these words to your partner.

  1. February

  2. Thursday

  3. August

  4. tomorrow

  5. year

  6. date

  7. birthday

  8. Saturday

  9. October

10. June

Listen to your partner. Write the word.

11. _____

12. _____

13. _____

14. _____

15. _____

16. _____

17. _____

18. _____

19. _____

20. _____

3.13 Spelling

Partner B

Listen to your partner. Write the word.

1. _____

2. _____

3. _____

4. _____

5. _____

6. _____

7. _____

8. _____

9. _____

10. _____

Spell these words to your partner.

11. September

12. January

13. Tuesday

14. month

15. calendar

16. yesterday

17. Friday

18. Sunday

19. clock

20. May

3.14 How old are you?

A: How old are you?
B: I'm 45 years old.

A: How old are you?
B: It's a secret.

A: How old are you?
B: I'd rather not say.

Ask your classmates their ages.

How old are you?   *I'm _____ years old.*

It's a secret.

I'd rather not say.

Name	Age

3.15 Writing

Write these numbers.

1. twenty-five   _____
2. eighty-one   _____
3. sixty-five   _____
4. fifty-six   _____

5. seventy-two   _____
6. thirty-nine   _____
7. forty-four   _____
8. ninety-seven   _____

3.16 Personal Information

Write about yourself.

Personal Information

Name: _____   **Date of Birth:** ___/___/___
          Last   First   Middle   Mo Day Yr

Address: _____   **Age:** _____
          Number   Street   Apartment

_____
          City   State   Zip Code

Telephone: _____   **Native Country:** _____
          Area Code   Number

Native Language: _____   **Nationality:** _____

Questions

What's your . . .?	What city do you live in?
first name	What country are you from?
last name	What language do you speak?
address	How do you spell that?
zip code	When is your birthday?
telephone number	How old are you?
nationality	

Ask your partner.

Personal Information

Name: _____   **Date of Birth:** ___/___/___
          Last   First   Middle   Mo Day Yr

Address: _____   **Age:** _____
          Number   Street   Apartment

_____
          City   State   Zip Code

Telephone: _____   **Native Country:** _____
          Area Code   Number

Native Language: _____   **Nationality:** _____

To the Teacher

Out and About is a beginning-level, activity-centered, multi-skills text designed to teach basic English and life skills to adult learners. It prepares students for survival in the classroom and in everyday situations outside of class.

OUTSTANDING FEATURES

- Can be used in multi-level low beginning classes (for example: true beginners, false beginners, and slower learners)
- Incorporates innovative practice activities
- Provides literacy support for students who need it
- Reinforces vocabulary in creative and stimulating ways
- Builds literacy skills while at the same time introducing students to more interesting and fun uses of the language
- Teaches study skills and stresses student responsibility
- Promotes communication in real-life situations
- Provides end-of-unit progress checks and self-monitoring progress charts
- Addresses SCANS competencies
- Meets CASAS requirements
- Celebrates the diversity of the language classroom and the world we live in*

* Out and About makes every effort to avoid stereotypes. In doing so, Out and About features people of various ethnic backgrounds, women in traditionally male occupations, and non-traditional families, such as single-parent families and same-sex couples. Students will also learn language for expressing food restrictions determined by religious custom or cultural preference.

COMPONENTS

Out and About is made up of three components: Student Book, Teacher's Guide, and a photocopy-ready Teacher Resource Book.

Student Book The Student Book consists of thirteen units, each focusing on a specific theme or set of themes related to everyday life. In each unit, topic-related vocabulary is introduced and practiced. The highly interactive activities are designed to address a range of learning styles and to provide practice in all skill areas: speaking, listening, reading, writing, and pronunciation. Included in the student book are pair work activities, interviews, class mingles, information gap activities, picture drawing, scrambled sentences, matching, and more. Most chapters conclude with a real-life task.

Teacher's Guide The Student Book is supported by the Teacher's Guide, which is well-organized and easy to use. The unit objectives, unit outline, and list of key vocabulary provided at the beginning of each unit allow for easy and thorough class preparation. Suggested procedures, stated in a clear step-by-step format, are easy to follow.

The Teacher's Guide is downloadable from the distributor's website, *www.altaesl.com*.

Teacher Resource Book The materials in the Teacher Resource Book are photocopy-ready and are designed to help maintain a lively atmosphere while minimizing the need for additional supplementation. Included in the Teacher Resource Book are supplementary games, crossword puzzles, class mingles, partner and whole-class information gap activities, fluency circles, double dictations, puzzles, end-of-unit progress checks, and more. The Teacher Resource Book can be used independently or in conjunction with the Student Book.

(Note: The Teacher Resource Book features its own teaching suggestions and answer keys.)

SUGGESTIONS FOR CLASSROOM USE

Vocabulary Presentation Vocabulary can be presented to the whole class either by using an overhead projector or by instructing students to look in their books. Elicit as much information as you can from the students, using as many different strategies as possible, for example: make drawings on the board; use gestures; supplement with pictures, photographs, and realia. Do not hesitate to try different strategies with different classes.

Mingles Mingles are designed to provide focused speaking practice with a large number of people. They are repetitive in nature and involve the skills of reading, writing, listening, and speaking. The classroom is generally noisy at this time, so students are less self-conscious about speaking English. Stop the activity when students have finished their worksheets or when you feel that they have received enough practice.

Pair work If possible, try to pair students from different language backgrounds. If you have an odd number of students, you will have to ask some students to form a group of three. You may want to choose three students who you think will complete the activity rather quickly so that they will finish at roughly the same time as the other students. Alternatively, you can choose to work with the extra student if you feel that you will not need to circulate among the other students.

Groupwork Depending on the makeup of your class, you may want to form new groups for each activity. This will allow students of different language backgrounds, proficiency levels, ages, and genders to work together.

Some activities focus on a specific skill and are marked by one of the three icons below.

 Listening   Reading   Writing

SCANS Competencies

Out and About fully integrates SCANS foundation skills and competencies. Activities are designed to develop learners' interpersonal skills, increase their sense of responsibility, enhance their self-esteem, provide learning strategies, and teach self-management. At the same time, these activities strengthen basic language and thinking skills.

While it was not practical for us to integrate the use of technology at this beginning level, we do suggest that learners be given responsibility for classroom duties such as turning on the audio equipment or overhead projector and using the copy machine to make copies.

Scope and Sequence

Unit	Topic	Functions
Getting Started page 1	Introductions	• Learning the names of classmates • Greeting and leave-taking • Developing interpersonal skills
Unit 1 page 3	In the Classroom	• Asking about items in the classroom • Understanding classroom instructions and vocabulary • Alphabet • Numbers 1–10 • Spelling
Unit 2 page 11	Nice to Meet You.	• Exchanging personal information • Filling out forms • Developing community • Numbers 11–100

Unit 3 page 19	What Day Is Today?	• Dates/days of the week
		• Months
		• Ordinal numbers
		• Personal information:
		    birthdays
		    telephone numbers
		    zip codes
		• Time

Unit 4 page 35	What Do You Do?	• Jobs • Identifying job skills/places of employment • Filling out schedules • Filling out applications
Unit 5 page 51	This Is My Family.	• Talking about families • Appreciating different types of families • Describing people
Unit 6 page 61	This Is My House.	• Talking about rooms/furniture • Talking about household chores • Location • *There is . . . /There are . . .* • The simple present • Discussing daily activities • Reading rental ads

Contents

3.17 What time is it? (Using *After*)

Listen to your teacher.

What time is it?

It's _____.

It's six o'clock.

It's six o' five.

It's five after six.

It's six ten.

It's ten after six.

It's six fifteen.

It's a quarter after six.

It's six twenty.

It's twenty after six.

It's six twenty-five.

It's twenty-five after six.

It's six thirty.

It's half-past six.

Write the times.

1. 7:05   _____
2. 10:10   _____
3. 8:25   _____
4. 12:15   _____
5. 3:20   _____

6. It's two-thirty.   _____
7. It's five after one.   _____
8. It's four ten.   _____
9. It's eleven o'clock.   _____
10. It's a quarter after two.   _____

3.18 What time is it? (Using *To*)

Listen to your teacher.

What time is it?

It's _____ .

It's six thirty.

It's six thirty-five.

It's twenty-five to seven.

It's six forty.

It's twenty to seven.

It's six forty-five.

It's a quarter to seven.

It's six fifty.

It's ten to seven.

It's six fifty-five.

It's five to seven.

It's seven o'clock.

Write the times.

1. 7:35   _____
2. 10:50   _____
3. 8:45   _____
4. 12:55   _____
5. 3:40   _____

6. It's two-forty.   _____
7. It's five to one.   _____
8. It's four fifty.   _____
9. It's nine o'clock.   _____
10. It's a quarter to two. _____

3.19 What time is it now?

Listen and circle the correct time.

1.	10:10	9:40
2.	9:15	8:45
3.	7:25	6:35
4.	3:20	2:40
5.	5:05	4:55
6.	1:25	12:35
7.	11:15	10:45
8.	9:20	8:40
9.	6:10	5:50
10.	10:05	5:10

Look at the clock. Write the time. Practice saying the time.

1.

_____

2.

_____

3.

_____

4.

_____

5.

_____

6.

_____

3.20 Telling Time: *After/To*

Complete the following with after *or* to.

1. 1:15

   It's a quarter _____ one.

2. 10:10

   It's ten _____ ten.

3. 7:35

   It's twenty-five _____ eight.

4. 12:05

   It's five _____ twelve.

5. 4:40

   It's twenty _____ five.

6. 12:45

   It's a quarter _____ one.

7. 9:50

   It's ten _____ ten.

8. 8:25

   It's twenty-five _____ eight.

9. 11:55

   It's five _____ twelve.

10. 5:20

   It's twenty _____ five.

Complete the following.

1. 8:40

   It's _____ to nine.

2. 12:55

   It's _____ to one.

3. 6:45

   It's _____ to seven.

4. 10:05

   It's _____ after ten.

5. 2:25

   It's _____ after two.

6. 9:20

   It's _____ after nine.

7. 1:05

   It's _____ after one.

8. 7:15

   It's _____ after seven.

9. 5:10

   It's _____ after five.

10. 1:35

   It's _____ to two.

3.21 Weekly Schedule

Fill in your weekly schedule. When do you do the following?

get up   work   sleep   do housework   do homework   study   relax   exercise

	Sun.	Mon.	Tues.	Wed.	Thurs.	Fri.	Sat.
1:00							
2:00							
3:00							
4:00							
5:00							
6:00							
7:00							
8:00							
9:00							
10:00							
11:00							
noon							
1:00							
2:00							
3:00							
4:00							
5:00							
6:00							
7:00							
8:00							
9:00							
10:00							
11:00							
midnight							

UNIT 4

What Do You Do?

4.1 Vocabulary Presentation

4.2 Speaking

PARTNER **A:** *Look at page 35.*

PARTNER **B:** *Look at page 36. Say the words.*

PARTNER **A:** *Point to the picture.*

Change roles and repeat.

She's a mechanic.

He's a cook.

She's a cashier.

He's a dishwasher.

She's a doctor.

She's a factory worker.

He's a gardener.

She's a server.

He's a painter.

4.3 Writing

Listen to your teacher. Write the words.

1. _____   3. _____   5. _____

2. _____   4. _____   6. _____

4.4 Complete the sentence.

1. _____ a mechanic.   4. _____ a doctor.

2. _____ a cook.   5. _____ a factory worker.

3. _____ a cashier.   6. _____ a gardener.

4.5 What do they do?

Listen to your teacher.

do/does	*is/are/am*
What *do I* do?	*I am* a mechanic.
What *do you* do?	*You are* a mechanic./*You are* mechanics.
What *does he* do?	*He is* a mechanic.
What *does she* do?	*She is* a mechanic.
What *do we* do?	*We are* mechanics.
What *do they* do?	*They are* mechanics.

What	do	I we	do?
		you they	
	does	he	
		she	

I	am	
You	are	
He	is	a mechanic.
She	is	
We	are	
You	are	mechanics.
They	are	

Complete the sentences.

1. What _____ you do?   I _____ a cook.

2. What _____ she do?   She _____ a housekeeper.

3. What _____ you do?   We _____ doctors.

4. What _____ they do?   They _____ students.

5. What _____ he do?   He _____ a cashier.

6. What _____ she do?   She _____ a server.

7. What _____ you do?   I _____ a seamstress.

8. What _____ he do?   He _____ a teacher.

9. What _____ she do?   She _____ a cook.

10. What _____ they do?   They _____ dishwashers.

4.6 Who are they?

Your teacher will give you some sentences. Match the sentences with the pictures. Write the sentences under the pictures.*

1.

2.

ALTA INTERNATIONAL INC.

3.

4.

5.

6.

*See the Teacher's Guide.

4.7 Reading and Writing

Reading 1

My name is Erika Jones.
I am a doctor. I work in a
hospital. I work from Sunday
to Thursday. I have Friday
and Saturday off. I work from
7 a.m. to 4 p.m. I like my
job very much.

I You We They	work
He She	works

Writing

Answer the questions.

1. What does Erika do? _____

2. Where does Erika work? _____

3. What days does she work? _____

4. What hours does she work? _____

Reading 2

My name is Jim Goldman. I am a server. I work in
a restaurant. I work from Thursday to Monday. I have
Tuesday and Wednesday off. I work from 4 p.m. to
midnight. I like my job very much.

Writing

Answer the questions.

1. Where does Jim work? _____

2. What does he do? _____

3. What days does he work? _____

4. What hours does he work? _____

4.8 Class Survey

What do you do?

What hours do you work?

What days do you work?

What days do you have off?

Ask your classmates.

Name	Job	Days	Hours	Days off

4.9   What does he do?/Where does she work?

Partner A

Tell your partner about these people.

He/She is a _____ .   He/She works _____ .

| Neil
nurse
in a hospital | Bill
baker
in a bakery | Francis
farmer
on a farm | Helen
homemaker
at home |

Ask your partner about these people.

What does _____ do?   Where does he work?

          Where does she work?

| Cari | Luke | Sally | Brenda |

How do you spell that?   Could you repeat that, please?

4.9 What does he do?/Where does she work?

Partner B

Ask your partner about these people.

What does _____ do?   Where does he work?

Where does she work?

Neil	Bill	Francis	Helen

Tell your partner about these people.

He/She is a _____ .   He/She works _____ .

Cari	Luke	Sally	Brenda
carpenter	letter carrier	seamstress	businessperson
at a construction site	at the post office	in a factory	in an office

How do you spell that?   Could you repeat that, please?

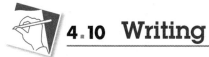

4.10 Writing

Look at pages 41–42. Write about these people.

1. Neil   _Neil is a nurse. He works in a hospital._

2. Bill   _____

3. Francis   _____

4. Helen   _____

5. Cari   _____

6. Luke   _____

7. Sally   _____

8. Brenda   _____

4.11 Talk to your classmates.

What do you do?   **Where do you work?**

Ask your classmates.

Name	Job	Place

4.12 What did you do?/What do you do?/What do you want to do?

I **was** a security guard.

I **am** a dishwasher now.

I **want to be** a police officer.

Draw a picture of your job in your country, your job now, and your job in the future.
Write about each one.

In My Country

_____

_____

_____

_____

Now

_____

_____

_____

_____

In the Future

_____

_____

_____

_____

4.13 Job Mingle

A: Hi Rafael. How are you?

B: Fine. How are you?

A: I'm fine, thanks. **What did you do** in Mexico?

B: I was a factory worker.

A: What do you do now?

B: I'm a cashier.

A: What do you want to be?

B: I want to be a mechanic.

A: Really? That's great. See you later.

B: See you.

What did you do in your country?	*I was a _____.*
What do you do now?	*I'm a _____.*
What do you want to be?	*I want to be a _____.*

Ask your classmates.

Name	Past Job	Present Job	Future Job

4.14 Our Jobs

Write about four classmates.

José is a student now. He was a carpenter in Mexico. He wants to be a computer programmer.

_____

_____

_____

_____

_____

_____

_____

_____

_____

_____

_____

4.15 My Partner's Schedule

Ask your partner about his or her weekly schedule. Fill in the calendar.

What time do you get up?   **What hours do you work?**   **What time do you go to bed?**
What days do you work?   **What hours do you go to school?**   **What days do you go to school?**

	Sun.	Mon.	Tues.	Wed.	Thurs.	Fri.	Sat.
1:00							
2:00							
3:00							
4:00							
5:00							
6:00							
7:00							
8:00							
9:00							
10:00							
11:00							
noon							
1:00							
2:00							
3:00							
4:00							
5:00							
6:00							
7:00							
8:00							
9:00							
10:00							
11:00							
midnight							

4.16 Find someone who . . .

Find someone for each of the following. Write their name.

1. _____   can drive a truck.

2. _____   can type fast.

3. _____   can cook.

4. _____   can trim trees.

5. _____   can drive a taxi.

6. _____   can take care of children.

7. _____   can serve in a restaurant.

8. _____   can use a computer.

9. _____   can wash dishes.

10. _____   can sew clothes.

11. _____   can plant trees and bushes.

12. _____   can use a cash register.

13. _____   can speak English.

14. _____   can build houses.

15. _____   can grow fruits and vegetables.

Can you . . .?

Do you know how to . . .?

4.17 What skills do you have?

Ask your partner about his or her skills. Make a list of his or her skills.

Can you . . .?

Do you know how to . . .?

_____

_____

_____

_____

_____

_____

4.18 My Partner's Skills

Write about your partner's skills.

_____

_____

_____

_____

_____

_____

_____

_____

_____

_____

This Is My Family.

5.1 Vocabulary Presentation

5.2 Speaking

PARTNER **A:** *Look at page 51.*

PARTNER **B:** *Look at page 52. Say the words.*

PARTNER **A:** *Point to the picture.*

Change roles and repeat.

family

father and daughter

mother and son

husband and wife

brother and sister

partners

boyfriend and girlfriend

grandmother and granddaughter

grandfather and grandson

 5.3 Writing

Listen to your teacher. Write the words.

1. _____   3. _____   5. _____

2. _____   4. _____   6. _____

 5.4 Partner to Partner

Say a word to your partner. Listen and write.

1. _____   3. _____   5. _____

2. _____   4. _____   6. _____

5.5 Ted's Family

Write these words on Ted's family tree.

brother daughter father mother sister son wife	Her name is . . . His name is . . .

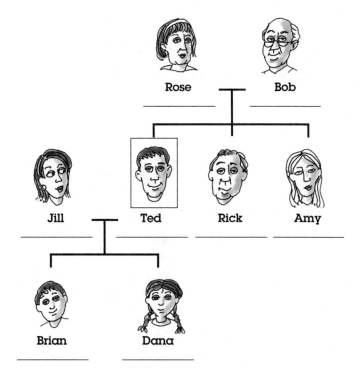

Answer the questions.

1. What is Ted's wife's name? _____

2. What is Ted's mother's name? _____

3. What is Ted's daughter's name? _____

4. What is Ted's sister's name? _____

5. What is Ted's father's name? _____

6. What is Ted's son's name? _____

7. What is Ted's brother's name? _____

5.6 This is my family.

Read about these families.

My name is Angela. This is my family. I am married with two children. My husband's name is Jake. We have two daughters. Their names are Tara and Marie.

My name is Valerie. I'm a single mother. I have one daughter. Her name is Lena. She is fourteen years old.

My name is David. I live with my partner Chip. We don't have any children. We have a dog. His name is Buddy.

Answer the questions.

1. How many children does Angela have? _____

2. How many children does Valerie have? _____

3. How many children do Chip and David have? _____

4. What are Angela's daughters' names? _____

5. What is Valerie's daughter's name? _____

6. What is Chip and David's dog's name? _____

7. How many children do you have? _____

5.7 She has two children.

I we	
you they	have
he	
she	has

I we	
you they	don't have
he	
she	doesn't have

1. Angela _____ two children.

2. Chip and David _____ a dog.

3. Valerie _____ a daughter.

4. Valerie _____ a son.

5. I _____ children.

6. I _____ brothers.

7. I _____ sisters.

8. I _____ a dog.

 ## 5.8 My Family

Write about your family.

_____

_____

_____

_____

_____

_____

_____

5.9 My Family Tree

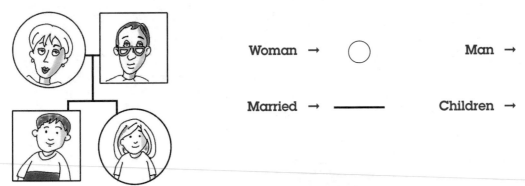

Draw your family tree.

Talk to your partner about your family.

This is my family.

This is my mother/father.

His/her name is _____.

I have _____ brothers/sisters/children.

I don't have any _____.

5.10 How many brothers and sisters do you have?

How many brothers do you have?   *I have* _____ *brother(s).*

How many sisters do you have?   *I have* _____ *sister(s).*

How many sons do you have?   *I have* _____ *son(s).*

How many daughters do you have?   *I have* _____ *daughter(s).*

                                        I don't have any _____ *. (brothers, sisters,*
                                        sons, daughters)

Ask your classmates.

Name	Brothers	Sisters	Sons	Daughters

5.11 Word Pairs

Complete the pairs.

1. mother and f _____

2. son and d _____

3. husband and w _____

4. brother and s _____

5. grandmother and g _____

5.12   What does she look like?

A: Do you know my brother?

B: What does he look like?

A: He's tall and thin. He has dark hair and a mustache.

B: Oh yes, I know him. He's handsome.

A: Do you know my sister?

B: What does she look like?

A: She's short and she has long brown hair.

B: No, I don't know her.

He is She is	tall	short	thin	heavy
	young	elderly	good-looking/ handsome	pretty/ beautiful

She has He has	short hair. long hair. straight hair. curly hair. wavy hair. brown hair. black hair. blond hair. red hair. dark hair. light hair.

She has He has	blue eyes. green eyes. hazel eyes. brown eyes. dark skin. light skin.
He has	a beard. a mustache. a goatee.

5.13 What do they look like?

Circle the correct word.

1. She has **straight/curly** hair.
   She has **light/dark** hair.
   She is **young/elderly**.

2. She is **beautiful/ugly**.
   She has **short/long** hair.
   She has **dark/light** hair.

3. He has **long/short** hair.
   He has **dark/light** hair.
   He has a **mustache/beard**.
   He is **heavy/thin**.

5.14 Find someone who . . .

Find someone for each of the following. Write their name.

1. _____ is tall.

2. _____ is short.

3. _____ is thin.

4. _____ is young.

5. _____ is handsome.

6. _____ is beautiful.

7. _____ has short hair.

8. _____ has long hair.

9. _____ has dark hair.

10. _____ has light hair.

11. _____ has a mustache.

12. _____ has a goatee.

13. _____ has curly hair.

14. _____ has straight hair.

15. _____ has brown eyes.

16. _____ has black hair.

17. _____ has blue eyes.

18. _____ has hazel eyes.

5.15 What does she look like?

Barbara and Carol are talking on the phone.

BARBARA: Hello.

CAROL: Hi, Barbara. This is Carol.

BARBARA: Oh, hi, Carol. How are you?

CAROL: I'm fine. How are you?

BARBARA: Just fine. What's up?

CAROL: Well, I have a small problem.

BARBARA: What is it?

CAROL: My sister and her kids are coming to visit me today. I have to work, so I can't pick them up at the bus station.

BARBARA: Oh, that's too bad. I can do it for you.

CAROL: Really? Are you sure?

BARBARA: Of course. What does your sister look like?

CAROL: She's short and a little heavy. She has long, dark, curly hair, dark eyes, and she wears glasses. She's very pretty. Her daughter is eight years old and her son is six.

BARBARA: What's her name?

CAROL: Her name is Ellen. Her daughter's name is Rena and her son's name is Alex.

BARBARA: What time do they arrive?

CAROL: At 4:26 p.m. Is that okay?

BARBARA: Yes, I'll be there.

CAROL: Thank you very much. You're a great friend.

Answer the questions.

1. Who is coming to visit Carol today?

_____

2. What time do they arrive?

_____

3. What is the problem?

_____

4. What is Barbara going to do?

_____

Draw a picture of Carol's sister.

This Is My House.

6.1 Vocabulary Presentation

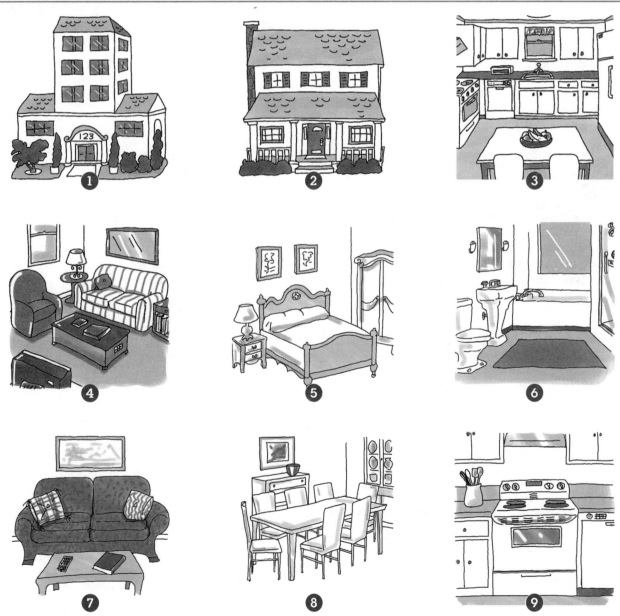

61

6.2 Speaking

PARTNER **A:** *Look at page 61.*

PARTNER **B:** *Look at page 62. Say the words.*

PARTNER **A:** *Point to the picture.*

Change roles and repeat.

I live in an apartment.

I live in a house.

This is the kitchen.

This is the living room.

This is the bedroom.

This is the bathroom.

There is a sofa in the living room.

There is a table in the dining room.

There is a stove and oven in the kitchen.

6.3 Writing

Listen to your teacher. Write the words.

1. _____   3. _____   5. _____

2. _____   4. _____   6. _____

6.4 Partner to Partner

Say a word to your partner. Listen and write.

1. _____   3. _____   5. _____

2. _____   4. _____   6. _____

6.5 Where We Live

Reading 1: My Apartment

My name is Aaron and this is my daughter, Tina. We live in an apartment in the city. We live on the 2nd floor. Our apartment has two bedrooms. It also has a living room, a bathroom, and a large kitchen. It's a nice place.

Writing

Answer the questions.

1. Who does Aaron live with? _____

2. Do they live in a house or an apartment? _____

3. Do they live in the city or in the suburbs? _____

4. How many bedrooms do they have? _____

5. Is there a living room in their apartment? _____

6. Is there a dining room in their apartment? _____

7. What floor do they live on? _____

Reading 2: My House

My name is Ann and this is my family. We live in a house in the suburbs. Our house has three bedrooms. There is a kitchen, living room, dining room, and two bathrooms. We also have a small yard. Our neighbors are very friendly. It's a great place.

Writing

Answer the questions.

1. Who does Ann live with? _____

2. Do they live in a house or an apartment? _____

3. Do they live in the city or in the suburbs? _____

4. Is there a dining room in their house? _____

5. How many bedrooms are there? _____

6. Do you live in a house or in an apartment? _____

7. Do you live in the city or in the suburbs? _____

8. How many bedrooms are there in your house/apartment? _____

9. What floor do you live on? _____

6.6 Where do we live?

Ask your classmates about their homes.

Do you live in a house or an apartment?

How many bedrooms are there?

Is there a living room?

Is there a dining room?

Is there a yard?

Yes, there is.

No, there isn't.

Name	House/Apt.	# of Bedrooms	Living Room	Dining Room	Yard
Ann	apartment	2	yes	no	no

6.7 This is my kitchen.

This is my kitchen. This is where I cook dinner.
I eat dinner with my family here. There is a refrigerator,
a stove, an oven, and a table and chairs. I wash dishes
in the sink.

refrigerator

stove and oven

table and chairs

Who cooks dinner in your house? _____

I You We They	cook dinner.

He She My husband My wife My partner	cooks dinner.

Ask your partner: Who cooks dinner in your house?

Who cooks dinner in your partner's house?

_____

6.8 What's in your kitchen?

Ask your partner about his/her kitchen. Write yes *or* no.

Is there	a refrigerator a stove a table a sink a dishwasher a window a TV a microwave oven	in your kitchen?	*Yes, there is.* *No, there isn't.*

Partner's name: _____

Refrigerator	Stove	Table	Sink
Dishwasher	**Window**	**TV**	**Microwave oven**

6.9 My Partner's Kitchen

Write about your partner's kitchen.

_____

_____

_____

_____

6.10 Who washes the dishes in your house?

I You We They	wash the dishes.	He She	washes the dishes.

Ask your classmates who cooks and washes the dishes.

Who cooks dinner in your house?　　*I do.*

Who washes the dishes?　　*My husband does.*

My wife does.

My son does.

My roommate does.

My friend does.

My friends do.

My partner does.

We all do.

Name	Cooks	Washes the dishes
Oscar	He does.	His sister does.

6.11 Spelling

I You We They	eat cook live **have** do go wash watch relax

He She	eat**s** cook**s** live**s** **has** do**es** go**es** wa**shes** wat**ches** rela**xes**

For verbs with **he** and **she**:	Add **s**.

Add **es** to words ending in **-ch**, **-sh**, **-x**, **-s**, **-z**, and with the words **do** and **go**.	*Examples:* wat**ches** wa**shes** rela**xes** pas**ses** do**es** go**es**

Complete the following sentences.

1. My husband _____ the dishes.

2. My roommate _____ dinner.

3. I _____ with my partner.

4. I _____ one brother and one sister.

5. After dinner we _____ TV.

6. My wife _____ in the living room after work.

7. My son _____ TV with his sister after school.

8. My family _____ dinner in the kitchen.

9. Our daughter _____ the dishes after dinner.

10. She _____ two children, a son and a daughter.

Add s *or* es *to the following.*

1. write____

2. teach____

3. brush____

4. work____

5. listen____

6. speak____

7. read____

8. kiss____

6.12 This is my living room.

This is my living room. This is where I relax and watch TV. There is a television and a sofa. There is also an easy chair and a lamp. My living room is very comfortable.

| easy chair/armchair | lamp | television (TV) |

Ask your classmates.

Is there a/an _____ in your living room?

Yes, there is.

No, there isn't.

Name	Sofa	TV	Lamp	Easy Chair

6.13 Where is it?

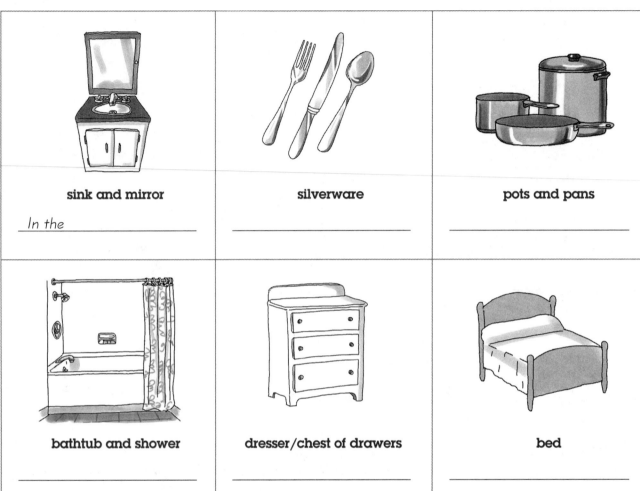

sink and mirror

In the _____

silverware

_____

pots and pans

_____

bathtub and shower

_____

dresser/chest of drawers

_____

bed

_____

Answer the questions.

1. Where do you sleep? _____

2. Where do you take a shower? _____

3. Where do you eat dinner? _____

4. Where do you watch TV? _____

5. Where do you brush your teeth? _____

6. Where do you listen to music? _____

7. Where do you get dressed? _____

8. Where do you read? _____

9. Where do you eat breakfast? _____

10. Where do you study? _____

6.14 Where does it go in the house?

Read each sentence.* Draw a picture or write the word.

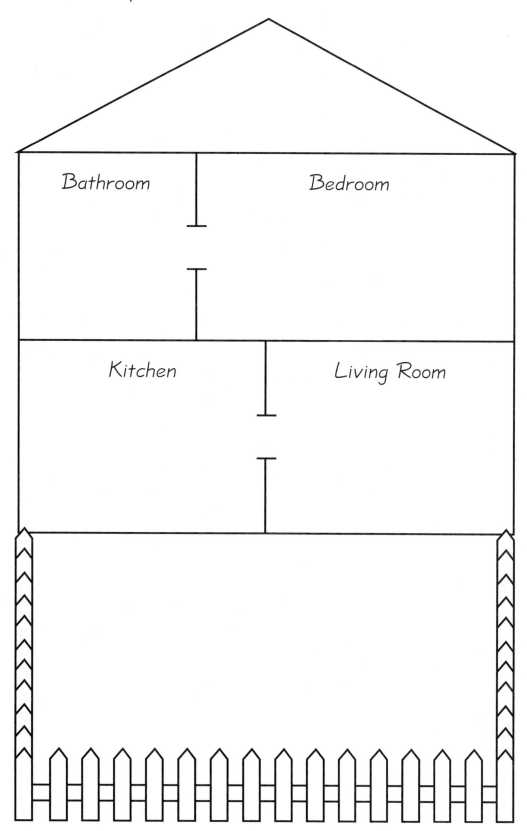

*See the Teacher's Guide.

6.15 Understanding Rental Ads

Abbreviations

br.   → bedroom   util.   → utilities*   *utilities = gas + electric (water, garbage)

l/r. → living room   incl.   → included

lrg. → large   trans. → transportation

d/r. → dining room   nr.   → near

mo.   → month   avail. → available

---

1. Civic Center

3 br. apt., lrg. kitchen, bath, patio, no pets or children, util. incl.
$2500/mo.

2. Mission

lrg. studio, big kitchen, quiet bldg., gas/electric incl., wood floors
$975/mo.

3. Richmond

2 br. apt., small kitchen, tile bath, old bldg., near park, pets ok
$1600/mo. + util.

4. Hayes Valley

1 br. apt., nice kitchen, tile bath, sunny, nr. shopping/trans.
$1200/mo. util. incl.

5. Chinatown

2 br. apt., nr. elementary school, quiet, sunny, clean, parking avail.
$1450/mo.

6. Diamond Heights

lrg. studio, nice view, quiet, clean bldg., parking incl.
$1150/mo. + util.

7. Haight Street

3 br. apt., small kitchen, l/r., d/r., yard, basement, pets ok, nr. park,
$2500/mo. + util.

8. Downtown

lrg. 2br. apt., large kitchen, d/r., l/r., balcony, pet ok, near bus, train
$2600/mo. + util.

Look at the apartment advertisements and answer the questions.

1. How many apartments have three bedrooms? _____

2. How many apartments have one bedroom? _____

3. How many houses are for rent? _____

4. How many studio apartments are for rent? _____

5. How many apartments have a balcony? _____

6. How many apartments are near the park? _____

7. How many apartments have a dining room? _____

8. Which apartments are good if you don't have a car? _____

9. How many apartments include utilities? _____

10. How many apartments have parking? _____

Help these people find an apartment. Write the number of the ad under the picture.

A. I'm single. I need a nice kitchen and a place to park my car. I also want a good view.

_____

B. We need a large apartment. We like to play in the park on weekends.

_____

C. We need a medium-sized apartment. We don't have a car. We take the bus to work.

_____

D. We want a one-bedroom apartment. We don't drive. We want to be near a shopping center.

_____

6.16 A Day in My House

Chris usually gets up at 6:00 every day. He takes a shower and shaves in the bathroom. He gets dressed in the bedroom. He has toast, fruit, and coffee for breakfast in the kitchen. After breakfast he washes the dishes and cleans the kitchen. At 7:30 he goes to work.

Chris gets home from work at 5:30. He washes his hands and face in the bathroom, and he changes his clothes in the bedroom. Then he cooks dinner in the kitchen. He eats dinner in the living room in front of the TV. After dinner he washes the dishes in the kitchen. Sometimes he listens to music, watches TV, or reads in bed before he goes to sleep.

What does Chris do in these places?

In the Bedroom

In the Bathroom

In the Kitchen

In the Living Room

What Do You Want to Eat?

7.1 Vocabulary Presentation

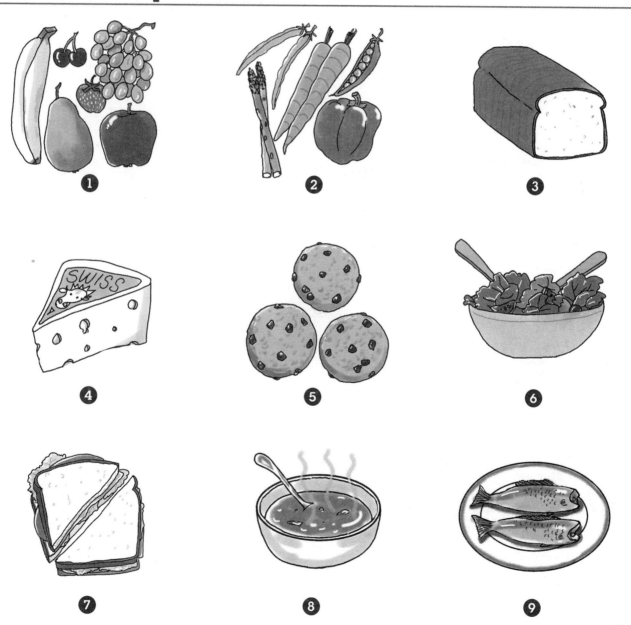

7.2 Speaking

PARTNER **A:** *Look at page 75.*

PARTNER **B:** *Look at page 76. Say the words.*

PARTNER **A:** *Point to the picture.*

Change roles and repeat.

fruit   vegetables

bread

cheese

cookies

salad

a sandwich

soup

fish

7.3 Writing

Listen to your teacher. Write the words.

1. _____   3. _____   5. _____

2. _____   4. _____   6. _____

7.4 Partner to Partner

Say a word to your partner. Listen and write.

1. _____   3. _____   5. _____

2. _____   4. _____   6. _____

7.5 Singular/Plural

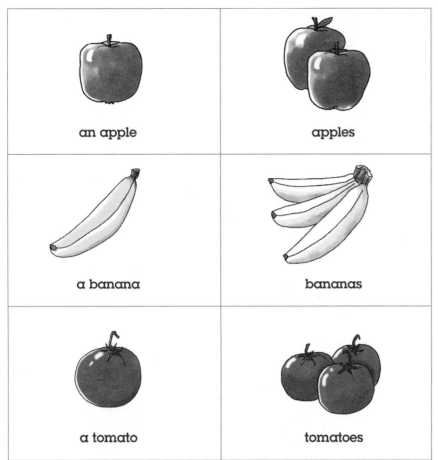

an apple	apples
a banana	bananas
a tomato	tomatoes

Complete the chart.

SINGULAR	PLURAL
an apple	apples
a cookie	_____
_____	oranges
a lemon	_____
a grape	_____
_____	carrots
_____	onions
a pepper	_____
_____	potatoes
_____	sandwiches
a hamburger	_____
_____	cakes

7.6 Making a Picture Dictionary

Draw pictures of fruits and vegetables. Ask your teacher or your partner, **"What's this called in English?"**
Write the word next to the picture.

A: What's this called in English?

B: It's corn. C - O - R - N

7.7 Count/Non-Count

Count	Non-count	
an apple/apples	corn	broccoli
an onion/onions	garlic	salt
a sandwich/sandwiches	bread	cheese
an egg/eggs	coffee	water
a potato/potatoes	milk	juice
a cookie/cookies	sugar	pepper

Is it count or non-count?

1. bananas _____

2. tea _____

3. cabbage _____

4. noodles _____

5. grapes _____

6. tomatoes _____

7. oranges _____

8. rice _____

7.8 What's the counter?

What can you buy in a _____? Write some examples.

bag	box	bottle	bunch	can	jar

pound	loaf	head	dozen	gallon

7.9 Do you need anything from the store?

A: Do you need anything from the store?

B: Yes, thanks. I need three tomatoes and a bunch of broccoli.

Ask your classmates, **"Do you need anything from the store?"** *Write their answers below. Look at your card.* * *Tell your classmates what you need.*

Name	Things from the Store

What's your name?   **Could you spell that, please?**

*See the Teacher's Guide.

7.10 At the Supermarket

Partner A

CLERK: Can I help you?

CUSTOMER: Yes, where are the apples?

CLERK: Apples are on aisle 1.

CUSTOMER: Okay, thanks.

> Where's . . .?
>
> Where are . . .?
>
> I'm looking for the . . .

CLERK: Can I help you?

CUSTOMER: Yes, where's the sugar?

CLERK: Sugar is on aisle 5.

CUSTOMER: Thank you.

Ask your partner about these things. Write them on the shelves below.

grapes	soy sauce	oranges
milk	garlic	canned corn
oil	tea	pasta

_____s are on aisle _____.   _____ is on aisle _____.

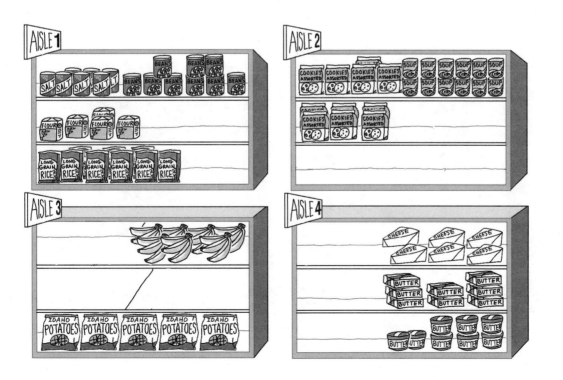

7.10 At the Supermarket

Partner B

CLERK: Can I help you?

CUSTOMER: Yes, where are the apples?

CLERK: Apples are on aisle 1.

CUSTOMER: Okay, thanks.

Where's . . .?
Where are . . .?
I'm looking for the . . .

CLERK: Can I help you?

CUSTOMER: Yes, where's the sugar?

CLERK: Sugar is on aisle 5.

CUSTOMER: Thank you.

Ask your partner about these things. Write them on the shelves below.

salt	flour	bananas
cookies	butter	rice
potatoes	soups	beans

_____s are on aisle _____. _____ is on aisle _____.

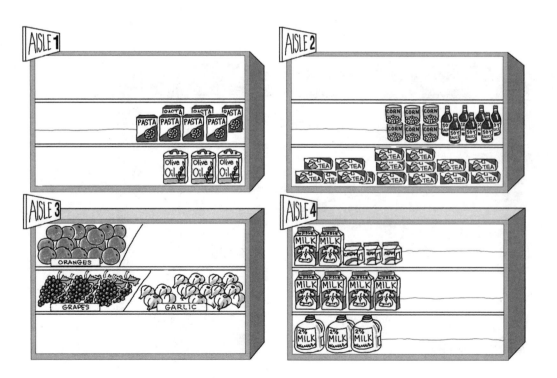

7.11 They're on aisle 2.

A: Excuse me, where are the cookies?

B: They're on aisle 4.

A: Thanks.

B: No problem.

A: Excuse me, where's the sugar?

B: It's on aisle 6.

A: Thank you very much.

B: You're welcome.

Ask your classmates about these items. Write the aisle number* in the right-hand column.

Item	Aisle
cookies	4
sugar	6
butter	
cabbage	
bread	
rice	
apples	
cheese	
orange juice	
potato chips	
soda	
tea	
napkins	
lettuce	
frozen peas	
chicken	
coffee	
soup	

*See the Teacher's Guide.

7.12 Do you eat meat?

Animal		Meat	
a cow		beef	
a pig		pork	
a chicken		chicken	
a fish		fish	
a sheep		lamb	

Do you eat beef?
Yes, I do.

Do you eat fish?
No, I don't.

Ask your partner. Write yes *or* no.

	Beef	Pork	Chicken	Fish
Your Partner				
You				

Food Restrictions

I don't eat meat. I'm vegetarian.

I don't eat beef. I'm Hindu.

I don't eat pork. I'm Muslim.

I'm allergic to shrimp.

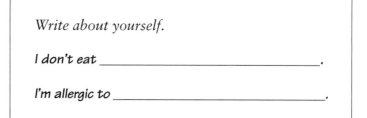

Write about yourself.

I don't eat _____.

I'm allergic to _____.

7.13 What kind of food do you like?

A: What kind of fruit do you like?

B: I like peaches.

A: What kind of vegetables do you like?

B: I like asparagus.

A: What kind of food do you like?

B: I like Chinese food.

Ask your classmates.

Name	Fruit	Vegetables	Food

What food is popular in your country? Ask five people from different countries. Write their answers.

Sushi is popular in Japan.

1. _____

2. _____

3. _____

4. _____

5. _____

7.14 What's in the refrigerator?

Look at your sentence strip.* Draw or write the food in the refrigerator.

*See the Teacher's Guide.

7.15 Breakfast, Lunch, and Dinner

I get up at 6:00. After I take a shower and get dressed, I eat breakfast with my family. We usually have fruit, coffee, and toast.

At 12:00 I eat lunch. I bring a sandwich, some carrots, and a piece of fruit to work. I usually eat lunch at my desk.

I eat dinner at home. We eat dinner at 7 p.m. Sometimes I cook dinner. Sometimes my partner cooks. We eat fish or chicken, vegetables, and a salad. We don't eat red meat.

1. What do you eat for breakfast? _____

2. What time do you have breakfast? _____

3. What do you eat for lunch? _____

4. What time do you have lunch? _____

5. What do you eat for dinner? _____

6. What time do you have dinner? _____

7.16 My Breakfast, Lunch, and Dinner

*Write about **your** breakfast, lunch, and dinner.*

_____

_____

_____

_____

_____

_____

_____

_____

_____

7.17 What do you eat?

What do you eat for (breakfast, lunch, dinner)?

What time do you eat (breakfast, lunch, dinner)?

Name	Breakfast	Time	Lunch	Time	Dinner	Time

7.18 Fruit Salad Recipe

Ingredients:

2 apples
2 bananas
1 orange
a bunch of grapes
a basket of strawberries
other fruit that you like

Wash all fruit. Peel the apples, cut them into bite-sized pieces, and put them in a large mixing bowl. Slice the bananas. Add them to the apples. Add the grapes to the apple/banana mixture. Cut the green part off the strawberries and throw it away. Slice the strawberries and add them to the bowl. Cut and add the other fruit. Mix carefully. Squeeze the orange over the fruit and mix again. Serve with mint leaves or yogurt. Enjoy!

7.19 Homework

Write a recipe from your culture. Ask your teacher to make copies for your classmates. Bring in food from you country. Share with your classmates!

8

How Much Is It?

8.1 Vocabulary Presentation

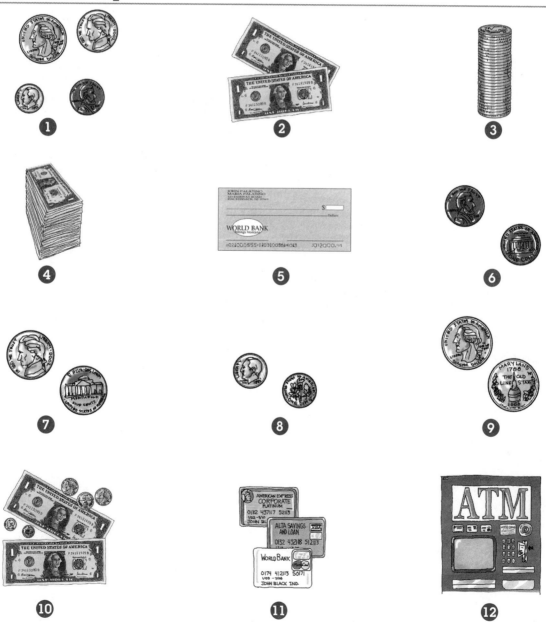

8.2 Speaking

PARTNER A: *Look at page 89.*

PARTNER B: *Look at page 90. Say the words.*

PARTNER A: *Point to the picture.*

Change roles and repeat.

cents

dollars

coins

bills

a check

a penny—1 cent

a nickel—5 cents

a dime—10 cents

a quarter—25 cents

cash

credit cards

ATM

8.3 Writing

Listen to your teacher. Write the words.

1. _____   3. _____   5. _____

2. _____   4. _____   6. _____

8.4 Partner to Partner

Say a word to your partner. Listen and write.

1. _____ 3. _____ 5. _____

2. _____ 4. _____ 6. _____

8.5 How much is it?

Match the amounts. Write the letter on the line.

_____ 1. 2 quarters   a. 50¢

_____ 2. 4 dimes   b. 1¢

_____ 3. 1 nickel   c. 25¢

_____ 4. 4 quarters   d. 10¢

_____ 5. 10 pennies   e. 20¢

_____ 6. 5 nickels   f. 40¢

_____ 7. 2 dimes   g. 5¢

_____ 8. 1 penny   h. $1.00

_____ 9. 5 quarters   i. 60¢

_____ 10. 6 dimes   j. $1.25

Write the amount.

1. 1 penny + 2 quarters =   ___51¢___

2. 2 dimes + 1 nickel =   _____

3. 4 pennies + 4 dimes =   _____

4. 1 penny + 1 nickel + 1 dime =   _____

5. 4 quarters =   _____

6. 2 nickels + 2 dimes + 2 quarters =   _____

7. 5 nickels + 3 quarters =   _____

8. 1 nickel + 1 dime + 1 quarter =   _____

9. 50 pennies + 1 nickel + 2 dimes + 1 quarter =   _____

10. 5 pennies + 5 nickels + 5 dimes + 1 quarter =   _____

Write the words for the money.

1. 1¢ _____   3. 50¢ _____   5.   25¢ _____

2. 10¢ _____   4.   5¢ _____   6. $1.00 _____

 ## 8.6 Prices

Listen and write the prices.

1.   ___$1.50___   3. _____   5. _____   7. _____

2. _____   4. _____   6. _____   8. _____

8.7 How much is . . .? / How much are . . .?

How much is coffee?	It's $6.99 a pound.
How much are bananas?	They're 79¢ a pound.

Complete the questions and answers.

1. _____ milk? _____ a gallon.

2. _____ bread? _____ a loaf.

3. _____ apples? _____ a pound.

4. _____ broccoli? _____ a bunch.

5. _____ rice? _____ a pound.

6. _____ eggs? _____ a dozen.

7. _____ lettuce? _____ a head.

8. _____ potatoes? _____ a pound.

9. _____ cookies? _____ a box.

10. _____ wine? _____ a bottle.

Check and compare your answers with a partner.

8.8 What's the price?

Look at your card.* Write the prices on your supermarket price sheet.
Ask your classmates for the other prices.

How much is . . .?   **How much are . . .?**

If you don't have the price, you can say, **"I'm sorry. I don't know."**

Supermarket Price Sheet

Item	Unit Price	Total
2 lbs. of oranges		
1 head of lettuce		
3 lbs. of apples		
2 lbs. of grapes		
1 bunch of broccoli		
2 lbs. of carrots		
5 lbs. of potatoes		
1 lb. of mushrooms		
2 bunches of celery		
2 lbs. of ground beef		
2 lbs. of chicken wings		
6 lbs. of lamb		
5 lbs. of turkey		
½ lb. of bacon		
3 lbs. of salmon		
2 lbs. of American cheese		

*See the Teacher's Guide.

8.9 Here's your change.

Partner A

CASHIER: That's $22.50.

CUSTOMER: Here's $25.00.

CASHIER: Your change is $2.50.
Thank you for shopping at Shop 'n' Save!

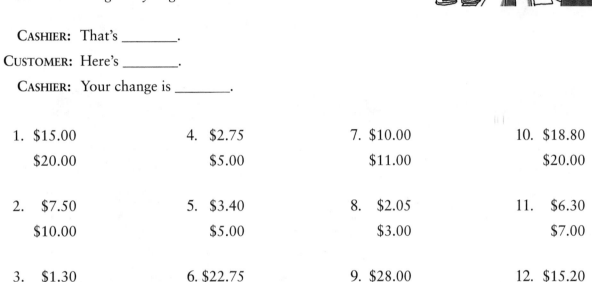

Practice this conversation with your partner.
How much change do you give?

CASHIER: That's _____.

CUSTOMER: Here's _____.

CASHIER: Your change is _____.

1. $15.00
   $20.00

2. $7.50
   $10.00

3. $1.30
   $1.50

4. $2.75
   $5.00

5. $3.40
   $5.00

6. $22.75
   $25.00

7. $10.00
   $11.00

8. $2.05
   $3.00

9. $28.00
   $30.00

10. $18.80
    $20.00

11. $6.30
    $7.00

12. $15.20
    $20.00

 8.10 Making Change

What coins do you need for the following amounts?

25¢ <u>2 dimes and a nickel</u> or <u>1 quarter</u>

1. 15¢ _____

2. 55¢ _____

3. 12¢ _____

4. 45¢ _____

5. 70¢ _____

6. 35¢ _____

7. 80¢ _____

8. 40¢ _____

9. 60¢ _____

10. 85¢ _____

8.11   How much do I owe?

Shop 'n' Save Supermarket
WEEKLY SAVINGS

3 lbs. 99¢

.59 lb.

.79 lb.

$1.49/bunch

99¢ lb.

$1.50 lb.

How much do I pay for the following things?

1. Two pounds of pears?   _____

2. Two pounds of cherries? _____

3. Three pounds of grapes? _____

4. Six pounds of oranges?   _____

5. Two bunches of broccoli? _____

6. Two pounds of bananas?   _____

You have $10.00. You want to buy fruit. What will you buy? Make a list.

_____   _____

_____   _____

8.12 This Week's Specials

Partner A

PRICE DOWN MARKET
This Week's Specials

apples 40¢/lb.

watermelon 30¢/lb.

strawberries $1.49/pint

bananas 19¢/lb.

grapes $1.29/lb.

How much is _____?

How much are _____?

Ask your partner about these things.

1. celery _____

2. mushrooms _____

3. cucumbers _____

4. tomatoes _____

5. corn _____

8.12 This Week's Specials

Partner B

PRICE DOWN MARKET
This Week's Specials

celery 49¢/lb.

mushrooms $2.49/lb.

corn 3/$1.00

tomatoes 4/$1.00

cucumbers 5/$1.00

How much is _____?

How much are _____?

Ask your partner about these things.

1. bananas _____

2. watermelon _____

3. apples _____

4. strawberries _____

5. grapes _____

8.13 How much is it?

Write the amount.

1. one twenty-dollar bill   _____

2. a ten-dollar bill, six quarters, two
   dimes, and two pennies   _____

3. a twenty-dollar bill, a five-dollar bill,
   two one-dollar bills, one quarter, and one nickel   _____

4. three twenty-dollar bills, a ten-dollar bill, two
   five-dollar bills, two quarters, and four pennies   _____

5. a five-dollar bill, two quarters, two nickels,
   and three dimes   _____

6. one five-dollar bill, one ten-dollar bill, four
   pennies, and one dime   _____

7. one twenty-dollar bill, three quarters, two dimes,
   two pennies, and three nickels   _____

8. four one-dollar bills, three five-dollar bills, twelve
   pennies, two quarters, and one nickel   _____

9. a five-dollar bill, three quarters, and five pennies   _____

10. one ten-dollar bill and three one-dollar bills   _____

8.14 Reading a Menu

The Country Kitchen Café

Appetizers

Soup of the day
    Bowl: $4.50
    Cup: $3.50

Green salad $5.00
Shrimp cocktail $6.50

Entrées

Hamburger..........................$8.25
Hot dog $5.75
Steak...................................$14.55
Grilled fish of the day $10.75
Grilled cheese sandwich $5.50
Ham and cheese sandwich $7.75

Fried chicken $7.75
Fried shrimp $8.95
Fried calamari $8.95
Fried fish of the day $10.25
Pasta of the day $10.25

Side orders

French fries $3.00
Potato salad $3.00
Pasta salad $3.00
Potato chips $3.00

Green beans $3.00
Corn-on-the-cob $3.00
Tomato salad.......................$3.00

Desserts

Cherry pie............................$4.25
Chocolate cake $4.25
Apple pie $4.25

Fruit salad $3.50
Ice cream $2.95

Beverages

Juice $3.00
Iced tea...............................$3.00
Iced coffee $3.50

Lemonade $3.00
Soda....................................$2.25
Hot tea or coffee $2.00

Look at the menu on page 100. Answer the following questions.

1. How much is a hamburger? _____

2. What do a hot dog, french fries, and a soda cost? _____

3. How much is a grilled cheese sandwich, lemonade, green beans, and a piece of chocolate cake? _____

4. How much is the pasta of the day, a green salad, and an iced tea? _____

5. How many desserts do they have? _____

6. How many salads do they have? _____

7. What is your favorite entrée? _____

8. What do you like to drink? _____

8.15 What do you want to eat?

Look at the menu again. What do you want to eat?

_____

_____

_____

_____

_____

_____

_____

_____

What Are You Wearing?

9.1 Vocabulary Presentation

9.2 Speaking

PARTNER **A:** *Look at page 103.*

PARTNER **B:** *Look at page 104. Say the words.*

PARTNER **A:** *Point to the picture.*

Change roles and repeat.

a shirt

a blouse

a skirt

a dress

a belt

a pair of pants

a pair of socks

a pair of shoes

a pair of sneakers

9.3 Writing

Listen to your teacher. Write the words.

1. _____   3. _____   5. _____

2. _____   4. _____   6. _____

9.4 Partner to Partner

Say a word to your partner. Listen and write.

1. _____   3. _____   5. _____

2. _____   4. _____   6. _____

9.5 What color is it?

Color in the squares.

white   black   gray   red   blue

green   yellow   orange   purple   brown

What color is it?

1. What color is a banana?   _____

2. What color is a strawberry?   _____

3. What color is an orange?   _____

4. What color is lettuce?   _____

5. What color are grapes?   _____

6. What color is a lemon?   _____

7. What color is broccoli?   _____

8. What color is your shirt today?   _____

9. What are you wearing today?   _____

10. What is your teacher wearing today?   _____

9.6 What's your favorite color?

Ask your classmates.

Name	What is your favorite color?	What color is your house?	What color is your bedroom?	What color are your eyes?

9.7 What are they wearing?

Partner A

Look at the pictures. Tell your partner what these people are wearing.

| Jane | Jack | Jessie | Jimmy |

Ask your partner what these people are wearing.

Betty	**Bob**	**Barbie**	**Billy**

9.7 What are they wearing?

Partner B

Ask your partner what these people are wearing.

Jane	Jack	Jessie	Jimmy

Look at the pictures. Tell your partner what these people are wearing.

Betty	Bob	Barbie	Billy

9.8 Where's my shirt?

Partner A

Where is my _____?	Where are my _____?

It's/They're   in

on

under

next to

Look at the picture of the bedroom. Answer your partner's questions.

Ask your partner where these things are. Draw them in the bedroom.

1. socks

2. jacket

3. shoes

4. skirt

9.8 Where's my shirt?

Partner B

Where is my _____?	**Where are my _____?**

It's/They're   in

on

under

next to

Ask your partner where these things are. Draw them in the bedroom.

1. sneakers

2. jeans

3. baseball cap

4. t-shirt

Look at the picture of the bedroom. Answer your partner's questions.

9.9 Find someone who . . .

Find someone for each of the following. Write their name.

1. _____ is wearing a white shirt.

2. _____ is wearing blue jeans.

3. _____ is wearing white socks.

4. _____ is wearing a green shirt.

5. _____ is wearing black shoes.

6. _____ is wearing a pair of sneakers.

7. _____ is wearing a sweatshirt.

8. _____ is wearing a jacket.

9. _____ is wearing a sweater.

10. _____ is wearing a belt.

11. _____ is wearing a blouse.

12. _____ is wearing a skirt.

13. _____ is wearing a baseball cap.

14. _____ is wearing a t-shirt.

9.10 What are your friends wearing?

Write about your classmates today.

1. _____ is wearing _____ .

2. _____ is wearing _____ .

3. _____ is wearing _____ .

4. _____ is wearing _____ .

5. _____ is wearing _____ .

9.11 Where are the men's shirts?

Partner A

A: Excuse me, where's the furniture?
B: Furniture is on the 6th floor.
A: Ok, thanks.

Ask your partner for the missing floor numbers.

A: **Excuse me, where is/are the _____?**

B: _____ is/are on the ____ floor/in the basement.

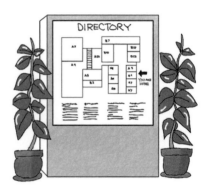

Maxie's Department Store	
Store Directory	
Department	**Floor**
Furniture	
Household Appliances	
Jewelry	1
Maxie's Café	
Maxie's Restaurant	7
Men's Casual Wear	
Men's Restroom	2, 4, Basement
Men's Shoes	2
Men's Sportswear	
Men's Suits	2
Men's Underwear	
Sale Items	Basement
Women's Casual Wear	4
Women's Dresses	
Women's Restroom	1, 3, 5
Women's Shoes	1
Women's Sportswear	4
Women's Underwear	

Read these sentences to your partner. Your partner will answer true or false.

1. Women's shoes and men's shoes are on different floors.

2. Women's underwear and women's sportswear are on the same floor.

3. Men's casual wear and men's shoes are on the same floor.

4. There is a women's restroom in the basement.

5. There is a restaurant on the 5th floor.

Listen to your partner. Your partner will read sentences to you. Answer and write T (true) or F (false) on the line.

6. _____   8. _____   10. _____

7. _____   9. _____

9.11 Where are the men's shirts?

Partner B

A: Excuse me, where's the furniture?
B: Furniture is on the 6th floor.
A: Ok, thanks.

Ask your partner for the missing floor numbers.

A: **Excuse me, where is/are**
the _____?

B: **_____ is/are on the ____**
floor/in the basement.

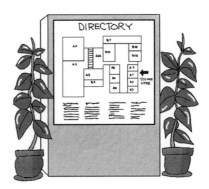

Department	Floor
Maxie's Department Store	
Store Directory	
Department	**Floor**
Furniture	6
Household Appliances	6
Jewelry	
Maxie's Café	Basement
Maxie's Restaurant	
Men's Casual Wear	3
Men's Restroom	2, 4, Basement
Men's Shoes	
Men's Sportswear	3
Men's Suits	
Men's Underwear	2
Sale Items	
Women's Casual Wear	
Women's Dresses	5
Women's Restroom	1, 3, 5
Women's Shoes	
Women's Sportswear	
Women's Underwear	4

Listen to your partner. Your partner will read sentences to you. Answer and write T *(true) or* F *(false) on the line.*

1. _____   3. _____   5. _____

2. _____   4. _____

Read these sentences to your partner. Your partner will answer true *or* false.

6. Women's dresses and women's shoes are on the same floor.

7. Men's underwear and men's sportswear are on the same floor.

8. Women's casual wear and women's shoes are on the same floor.

9. There is a men's restroom in the basement.

10. There is a cafe on the 2nd floor.

9.12 Reporting a Crime

Sarah is walking to the grocery store on a Saturday afternoon. She has her purse hanging from her shoulder. Suddenly, a man runs up behind her, grabs her purse, and runs away. She runs to a pay phone and calls 911. Here is what she says:

DISPATCHER: 911. What are you reporting?

SARAH: A man is running away with my purse! Help me!

DISPATCHER: Where are you?

SARAH: I'm on Ocean Avenue near the supermarket.

DISPATCHER: A police car is on its way. What does the man look like?

SARAH: He's tall and thin. He's Caucasian.

DISPATCHER: What's he wearing?

SARAH: I'm not sure. I think he's wearing jeans and a white t-shirt. He's wearing white sneakers.

DISPATCHER: What color hair does he have?

SARAH: He has long, brown hair and a beard.

DISPATCHER: How old is he?

SARAH: He's young, around 20 or 25.

DISPATCHER: Is he alone?

SARAH: Yes.

DISPATCHER: We're looking for him now. Stay where you are. A police car will be there soon.

SARAH: Thank you.

DISPATCHER: Goodbye.

SARAH: Goodbye.

Complete the sentences.

1. A man takes Sarah's _____.	purse/wallet
2. Sarah calls _____.	an ambulance/the police
3. Sarah _____ money into the telephone before she calls 911.	puts/doesn't put
4. The dispatcher asks Sarah to _____.	stay by the telephone/go home

9.13 Describing a Suspect

Write a description of the person who took Sarah's purse.

_____

_____

_____

_____

_____

Look at the police line-up. Can you find the man who took Sarah's purse?

 ## 9.14 Find the Suspect

Walk around. Don't show your card* to anyone. Talk to your classmates. Find a matching card.
When you think you have a match, call your teacher.

A: I'm looking for a man.

B: What does he look like?

A: <u>He's tall and thin. He's about 45 years old. He's of average height.</u>

B: What's he wearing?

A: <u>He's wearing a white t-shirt, blue jeans, and sneakers.</u>

B: No, I didn't see him./Yes, here he is.

*See the Teacher's Guide.

9.15 Contact Assignment

Go to a department store. Look at the directory. Write down the floor numbers.

Name and address of your department store: _____

_____

_____

Department	Floor	Department	Floor
Shoes		Hosiery	
Children's Clothing		Men's Formal Wear	
Cosmetics		Women's Sportswear	
Furniture		Restrooms	
Luggage		Customer Service	

Write about the department store.

Perry's Department Store has chairs, sofas, tables, and lamps. The furniture is on the 2nd floor.

_____

_____

_____

_____

_____

_____

9.16 Small Group Discussion

Write down three questions to ask your classmates about the department store.

_____

_____

_____

Ask and answer questions with your group. Do not write down the answers.

UNIT 10

Places in the Community

10.1 Vocabulary Presentation

1

2

3

4

5

6

7

8

9

10.2 Speaking

PARTNER **A**: *Look at page 117.*

PARTNER **B**: *Look at page 118. Say the words.*

PARTNER **A**: *Point to the picture.*

Change roles and repeat.

bank

supermarket

post office

drugstore

hospital

restaurant

school

park

laundromat

10.3 Writing

Listen to your teacher. Write the words.

1. _____

3. _____

5. _____

2. _____

4. _____

6. _____

10.4 Partner to Partner

Say a word to your partner. Listen and write.

1. _____

3. _____

5. _____

2. _____

4. _____

6. _____

10.5 Name that place.

Look at the map. Read the descriptions. Write the names of the places.

1. The park is in the middle of town.

2. The post office is across from the park.

3. The supermarket is between the laundromat and the hardware store.

4. The parking lot is next to the computer store.

5. The drugstore is across from the art studio.

6. The bank is behind the department store.

7. The hospital is next to the bank.

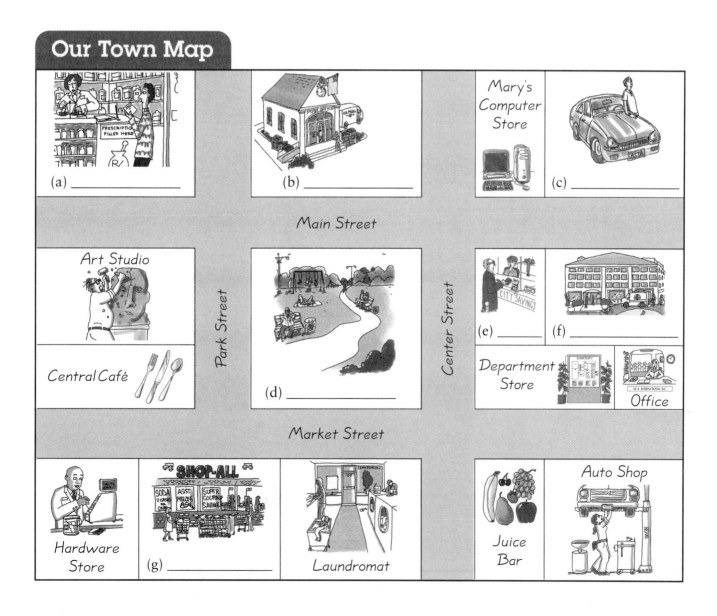

10.6 At the Bank

I have two bank *accounts* at the Bank of California. I have a *savings account* and a *checking account*. I use my savings account to keep money for the future. I use my checking account to pay my bills every month. Sometimes I use the *ATM* on the street, or sometimes I go into the bank and talk to a *teller*. I can *deposit* money into my accounts or *withdraw* money from my accounts. I can also *check my balance* to see how much money I have. My grandmother keeps her money in her kitchen, but I like my bank. My bank can *cash a check*, but my grandmother's kitchen can't.

Complete the sentences.

1. I keep my money to pay the bills in a _____.

2. I keep my money for the future in a _____.

3. A machine on the street where I can get money is an _____.

4. A person who works at a bank is called a _____.

5. When I put money into my account, I _____ it.

6. When I take money out of my account, I _____ it.

7. To see how much money I have in the bank, I _____.

8. To get money for a check at the bank, I _____.

10.7 Writing Checks

Listen to your teacher. Fill out the checks.

	101
	Date _____
Pay to the order of _____ $ [____]	
_____ dollars	
Memo _____ _____	
1:12345678': 00000000000'0101	

	102
	Date _____
Pay to the order of _____ $ [____]	
_____ dollars	
Memo _____ _____	
:345678': 00000000000'0102	

	103
	Date _____
Pay to the order of _____ $ [____]	
_____ dollars	
Memo _____	
1:12345678': 00000000000'0103	

10.8 Where do you keep your money?

Ask four classmates.

Name	Where do you keep your money?	Do you have a checking account?	Do you have a savings account?	Do you use an ATM?

10.9 Filling Out Bank Forms

1. Fill out this deposit slip for $100 in cash and a check for $50.

DEPOSIT TICKET

Cash ▶

Date _____

≪ **My Bank** ≫

Account Number

$

1 : 1 2 3 4 5 6 7 8 ' : 0 0 0 0 0 0 0 0 0

2. Fill out this withdrawal slip for $50.

WITHDRAWAL TICKET

Date _____

Name _____

Account Number

Amount _____ $

≪ **My Bank** ≫

1 : 1 2 3 4 5 6 7 8 ' : 0 0 0 0 0 0 0 0 0

10.10 At the Supermarket

Every Saturday I go to the supermarket to buy groceries. I buy groceries for my family for one week.

First I get a shopping cart at the entrance to the supermarket. I push my cart and begin in the *produce section*. I look for fresh fruit and vegetables. I like to buy oranges, apples, grapefruits, lettuce, and carrots.

After I leave the produce section, I go to the *meat department*. I buy some beef or pork. Sometimes I buy lamb.

Next to the meat department is the *poultry section*. I usually buy chicken, but sometimes I buy turkey.

My husband likes fish, so I go to the *seafood department* to buy fresh fish. Then I pick up some bread from the *bakery*.

I walk up and down the aisles of the supermarket and buy what I need for my family. When I get to the *dairy section*, I buy milk, butter, eggs, and cream. Before I go to the cashier, I stop at the *frozen foods section*. Sometimes I buy ice cream, frozen vegetables, or frozen dinners.

Finally, I go to the *checkout* and wait in line to pay the cashier. I pay for my groceries and go home.

Answer the questions.

1. When does this person go to the supermarket?   _____

2. What does she buy first?   _____

3. Where does she find fruit and vegetables?   _____

4. Does she buy fish in the meat department?   _____

5. Where does she find chicken?   _____

6. What does she buy in the dairy section?   _____

10.11 What's in this section?

Work with a partner. What foods are in each section?
Write three foods that you know.

Produce _____ _____ _____

Meat _____ _____ _____

Poultry _____ _____ _____

Dairy _____ _____ _____

Frozen Foods _____ _____ _____

Seafood _____ _____ _____

Bakery _____ _____ _____

10.12 Label the sections.

Work with a partner. Label the sections. Use these words.

bakery	dairy	frozen foods	meat
poultry	produce	seafood	

10.13   What do you usually buy in the _____ section?

A: Robert, what do you usually buy in the dairy section?

B: Yogurt.

A: What do you buy in the produce section?

B: Apricots.

Ask your classmates what they usually buy from each section. Name one food that you buy.

Name	Dairy	Produce	Poultry	Seafood

10.14 At the Post Office

Do you know these things? With a partner, write the words that you know.

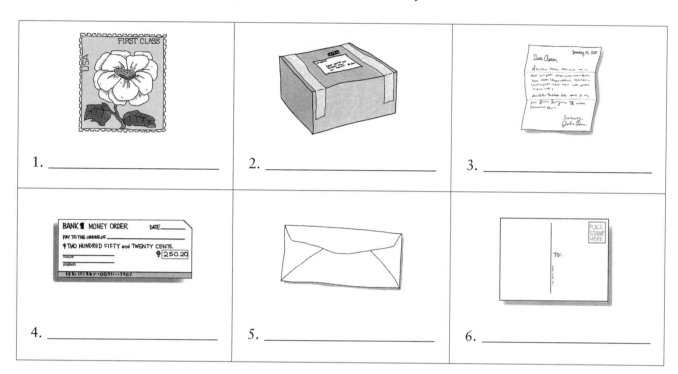

1. _____

2. _____

3. _____

4. _____

5. _____

6. _____

Practice this conversation with your teacher. Then practice with a partner.

CLERK: Next in line! May I help you?

CUSTOMER: Yes, I'd like to mail this package.

CLERK: Okay, that's $3.65.

CUSTOMER: Here you are.

CLERK: Would you like a receipt?

CUSTOMER: Yes, please.

CLERK: Here you are. Thank you. Next!

Would you like a receipt?

Yes, please.   *No, thanks.*

Partner A	**Partner B**
1. You are a customer at the post office. Your partner is the clerk. Make three conversations. You want to: ■ buy a money order ■ mail a postcard ■ send a package 2. You are a clerk at the post office. Your partner is the customer. Make three conversations.	1. You are a clerk at the post office. Your partner is the customer. Make three conversations. 2. You are a customer at the post office. Your partner is the clerk. Make three conversations. You want to: ■ buy stamps ■ mail a letter ■ pick up a package

10.15 Addressing an Envelope

Ask your classmates.

First Name	Last Name	Address	Zip Code

Write one classmate's name and address in the center of the envelope. Write your name and address in the upper left-hand corner of the envelope.

Look at the envelope. Answer the questions, true *or* false.

Robert Smith
195 Lakeview Ave.
Chicago, IL 60609

        Rita Phillips
        256 Market Street
        Philadelphia, PA 19102

_____ 1. The letter is going to Chicago.

_____ 2. The letter is coming from Chicago.

_____ 3. Robert Smith is sending the letter.

_____ 4. Rita Phillips is going to receive the letter.

_____ 5. Robert Smith's zip code is 19102.

_____ 6. Rita Phillips lives on Market Street.

10.16 Places in the Neighborhood

Ask your classmates these questions. Write their names and answers.

Question	Name	Answer
What's a cashier?	Roberta	the person you give money to when you buy something

Question	Name	Answer
1. Where can I cash a check?	_____	_____
2. What are dairy products?	_____	_____
3. What can I buy in the frozen foods section?	_____	_____
4. What does *deposit* mean?	_____	_____
5. Name a supermarket.	_____	_____
6. How much is a quart of milk?	_____	_____
7. What can I buy in the bakery?	_____	_____
8. What is *poultry*?	_____	_____
9. What is an *ATM*?	_____	_____
10. What can I buy in the produce department?	_____	_____

10. 17 At the Drugstore

Match the picture with the word.

_____ 1. soap

_____ 2. shampoo

_____ 3. medicine

_____ 4. greeting card

_____ 5. shopping basket

_____ 6. shaving cream

_____ 7. candy

_____ 8. photo lab

_____ 9. toothpaste

_____ 10. makeup

10. 18 Contact Assignment

Go to your drugstore and answer these questions.

Yes, it does.   **No, it doesn't.**

1. Does your drugstore sell greeting cards?   _____

2. Does your drugstore have an ATM?   _____

3. Does your drugstore sell candy?   _____

4. Does your drugstore have a photo lab?   _____

5. Does your drugstore sell makeup?   _____

6. Does your drugstore sell shampoo?   _____

7. Does your drugstore sell pencils?   _____

10.19 Where is it?

Partner A

CLERK: Can I help you?

CUSTOMER: Yes, where's the shampoo?

CLERK: The shampoo is on aisle 1.

CUSTOMER: Okay, thanks.

CLERK: Can I help you?

CUSTOMER: Yes, I'm looking for greeting cards.

CLERK: Greeting cards are on aisle 2.

CUSTOMER: Thank you.

Ask your partner about these things. Write them on the shelves below.

batteries	diapers	makeup
paper towels	sunscreen	pencils
film	soap	vitamins

_____s are on aisle _____.   _____ is on aisle _____.

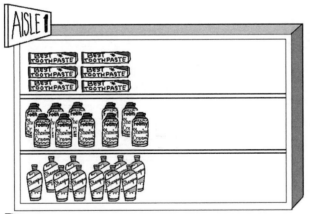

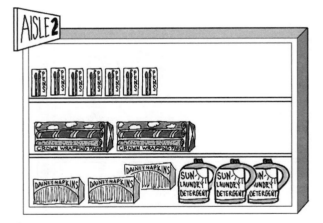

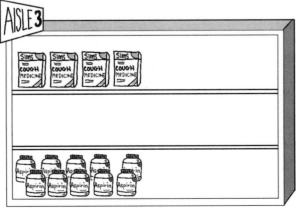

10.19 Where is it?

Partner B

CLERK: Can I help you?

CUSTOMER: Yes, where's the shampoo?

CLERK: The shampoo is on aisle 1.

CUSTOMER: Okay, thanks.

CLERK: Can I help you?

CUSTOMER: Yes, I'm looking for greeting cards.

CLERK: Greeting cards are on aisle 2.

CUSTOMER: Thank you.

Ask your partner about these things. Write them on the shelves below.

napkins	wrapping paper	shampoo
pens	shaving cream	cough medicine
toothpaste	aspirin	laundry detergent

_____s are on aisle _____.   _____ is on aisle _____.

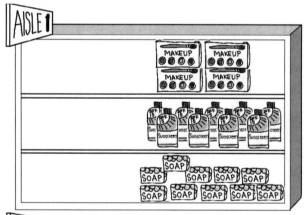

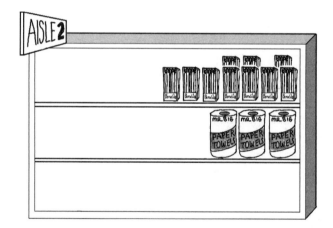

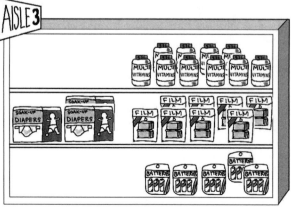

10.20 Personal Hygiene Products: Brand Names

A: What brand of *soap* do you use?

B: I use *Soapy Soap*.

Ask your classmates.

Name	Soap	Toothpaste	Shampoo

10.21   Where can you do these things?

Where can you _____?

at the bank   at the post office   at the supermarket   at the drugstore

at the laundromat   at the hospital   at the park   at school

Walk around and ask your classmates.

1. mail a letter   _____

2. wash your clothes   _____

3. see a doctor   _____

4. eat lunch   _____

5. relax   _____

6. buy fruit   _____

7. study Spanish   _____

8. get money   _____

9. cash a check   _____

10. open an account   _____

11. buy greeting cards   _____

12. buy fish   _____

13. buy toilet paper   _____

14. pick up a package   _____

15. check your balance   _____

10.22 What are you going to do tomorrow?

Read your card.* Make a sentence.

Example:

> buy shampoo

I'm going to buy shampoo at the supermarket.

Walk around and ask your classmates, **"What are you going to do tomorrow?"**
Write their answers.

    Rick is going to buy shampoo at the supermarket.

1. _____

    _____

2. _____

    _____

3. _____

    _____

4. _____

    _____

5. _____

    _____

6. _____

    _____

7. _____

    _____

*See Teacher's Guide.

I'd Like to Make An Appointment.

11.1 Vocabulary Presentation

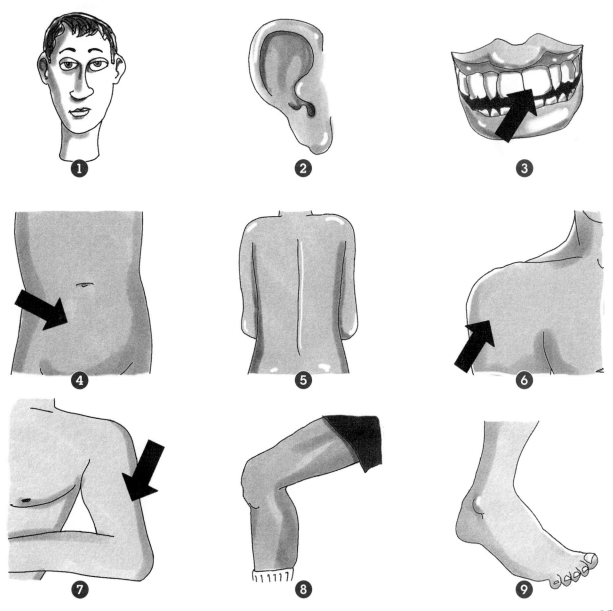

11.2 Speaking

PARTNER **A:** *Look at page 135.*

PARTNER **B:** *Look at page 136. Say the words.*

PARTNER **A:** *Point to the picture.*

Change roles and repeat.

head

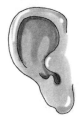

ear

tooth

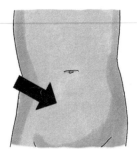

stomach

back

shoulder

arm

leg

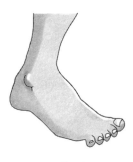

foot

11.3 Writing

Listen to your teacher. Write the words.

1. _____   3. _____   5. _____

2. _____   4. _____   6. _____

11.4 Partner to Partner

Say a word to your partner. Listen and write.

1. _____   3. _____   5. _____

2. _____   4. _____   6. _____

11.5 Does it hurt?

Partner A

1. *Your partner will tell you what hurts. Listen, touch that part of your body, and show pain on your face. Try to make your partner laugh!*

2. *Say these sentences to your partner one at a time. Watch your partner's face.*

   I have a headache.   My shoulder hurts.

   I have an earache.   My foot hurts.

   I have a stomachache.   My neck hurts.

Partner B

1. *Say these sentences to your partner one at a time. Watch your partner's face.*

   I have a backache.   My arm hurts.

   I have a headache.   My shoulder hurts.

   I have a toothache.   My leg hurts.

2. *Your partner will tell you what hurts. Listen, touch that part of your body, and show pain on your face. Try to make your partner laugh!*

11.6 Making an Appointment

RECEPTIONIST: Hello, Dr. Jones' office.

PATIENT: Yes, I'd like to make an appointment.

RECEPTIONIST: How about tomorrow at 10:00?

PATIENT: That's fine.

RECEPTIONIST: May I have your name, please?

PATIENT: Yes, this is Victor Hayes.

RECEPTIONIST: Could you spell that, please?

PATIENT: Yes, it's H – A – Y – E – S.

RECEPTIONIST: And what's the problem, Mr. Hayes?

PATIENT: I have an earache.

RECEPTIONIST: Okay, we'll see you tomorrow at 10:00.

PATIENT: Okay, thank you very much.

I have an earache.	My arm hurts.
I have a stomachache.	My leg hurts.
I have a headache.	My shoulder hurts.
I have a backache.	My foot hurts.
I have a toothache.	My head hurts.

Make a conversation with your partner.

RECEPTIONIST: Hello, doctor's office.

PATIENT: Yes, I'd like to make an appointment.

RECEPTIONIST: When can you come in?

PATIENT: How about _____?

RECEPTIONIST: That's fine. May I have your name, please?

PATIENT: _____.

RECEPTIONIST: And what's the problem?

PATIENT: _____.

RECEPTIONIST: Okay, we'll see you at _____.

PATIENT: Okay, thank you very much.

11.7 I'd like to make an appointment.

A: Hello. I'd like to make an appointment. **B:** When can you come in? **A:** How about *Tuesday* at *4 o'clock*? **B:** That's fine. We'll see you then.	**A:** Hello. I'd like to make an appointment. **B:** When can you come in? **A:** How about *Wednesday* at *3 o'clock*? **B:** I'm sorry, but the doctor is busy at that time. How about *Wednesday* at *2 o'clock*? **A:** Yes, that's fine.

Make appointments with your classmates. Fill in your calendar.

Monday	Tuesday	Wednesday	Thursday	Friday
9:00	9:00	9:00	9:00	9:00
10:00	10:00	10:00	10:00	10:00
11:00	11:00	11:00	11:00	11:00
Lunch	Lunch	Lunch	Lunch	Lunch
1:00	1:00	1:00	1:00	1:00
2:00	2:00	2:00	2:00	2:00
3:00	3:00	3:00	3:00	3:00
4:00	4:00	4:00	4:00	4:00

11.8 I have a cold.

RECEPTIONIST: Hello, City English School.

STUDENT: Hello, this is Mark Santos. I can't come to class today.

RECEPTIONIST: What's the matter?

STUDENT: I have a cold.

RECEPTIONIST: Okay, Mark, what class are you in?

STUDENT: I'm in Level 1.

RECEPTIONIST: Who's your teacher?

STUDENT: Mr. Green.

RECEPTIONIST: What time is your class?

STUDENT: It's at 2:00 in room 308.

RECEPTIONIST: Okay, Mark, we'll tell Mr. Green that you're sick.

STUDENT: Thank you.

Answer the questions.

1. What's wrong with Mark?   _____

2. What class is he in?   _____

3. Who is his teacher?   _____

4. What time is his class?   _____

5. What room is his class in?   _____

    ....

6. What is your teacher's name?   _____

7. What class are you in?   _____

8. What time is your class?   _____

9. What is the number of your classroom?   _____

10. What is the telephone number of your school? _____

Practice with your teacher. Practice with a partner.

I have a cold. I have a fever. I have a sore throat.	My son is sick. My husband is sick. My wife is sick. My partner is sick. My daughter is sick.	I feel dizzy. I feel nauseous.

11.9 Can I take a message?

Partner A

1. You are a student. Your partner is the school secretary. You are sick today.
    Call the school secretary. Tell her that you will be absent.

2. You are the school secretary. Answer the telephone and take a message.

MESSAGE	
	Date: _____
Name: _____	Class: _____
Teacher: _____	Room: _____
Reason for Absence: _____	

11.10 I'm sick today.

Partner A

1. These students are absent from school today. Ask your partner why they are absent.

What's the matter with _____?   **What's wrong with _____?**

Carla has a sore throat.

Elizabeth _____.   Joan _____.

Anna _____.   Steve _____.

Paul _____.   Mark _____.

Lori _____.   Silvia _____.

Mike _____.

2. Answer your partner's questions.

He has . . . /She has . . .   **He is . . . /She is . . .**   **He feels . . . /She feels . . .**

He has . . . /She has . . .	He is . . . /She is . . .	He feels . . . /She feels . . .
Kathie has an earache.	Leo's daughter is sick.	Al feels nauseous.
Evan has a fever.	Teresa feels dizzy.	Sonia's husband is sick.
Nicholas has a cold.	Phillip's son is sick.	Ryan's partner is sick.

11.9 Can I take a message?

Partner B

1. *You are the school secretary. Answer the telephone and take a message.*

> **MESSAGE**
>
> Date: _____
>
> Name: _____   Class: _____
>
> Teacher: _____   Room: _____
>
> Reason for Absence: _____

2. *You are a student. Your partner is the school secretary. You are sick today.*
    Call the school secretary. Tell her that you will be absent.

11.10 I'm sick today.

Partner B

1. *Answer your partner's questions.*

He has . . . /She has . . .	He is . . . /She is . . .	He feels . . . /She feels . . .
Mark has a headache.	Paul's partner is sick.	Silvia feels nauseous.
Lori has a cold.	Elizabeth feels dizzy.	Anna's son is sick.
Mike's wife is sick.	Steve's daughter is sick.	Joan has a fever.

2. *These students are absent from school today. Ask your partner why they are absent.*

What's the matter with _____?   **What's wrong with _____?**

Carla has a sore throat.

> Kathie _____.   Nicholas _____.
>
> Teresa _____.   Al _____.
>
> Sonia _____.   Leo _____.
>
> Evan _____.   Ryan _____.
>
> Phillip _____.

11.11 What's the matter?/What's wrong?

Practice these conversations.

A: What's the matter?	**A:** What's wrong?	**A:** What's the matter?
B: I have a headache.	**B:** My foot hurts.	**B:** I feel dizzy.
A: Oh, I'm sorry to hear that.	**A:** Oh, I'm sorry to hear that.	**A:** Oh, I'm sorry to hear that.

Look at your card.* Write the problem here.

_____

Walk around the room. Write down the problems with your classmates.

> Bonnie has a headache.
> John's foot hurts.
> Lee feels dizzy.

1. _____

2. _____

3. _____

4. _____

5. _____

6. _____

7. _____

8. _____

9. _____

10. _____

*See the Teacher's Guide.

11.12 The Body

Work with a partner. Write the parts of the body that you know.

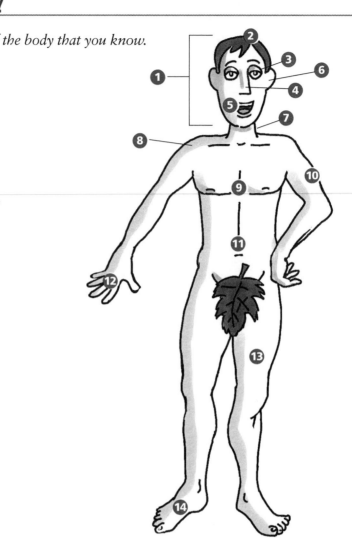

1. _____
2. _____
3. _____
4. _____
5. _____
6. _____
7. _____
8. _____
9. _____
10. _____
11. _____
12. _____
13. _____
14. _____

11.13 Touch your toes!

Tell your partner to touch parts of his/her body.

For example:

A: Touch your shoulder.

B: (Touches her shoulder.)

A: Good! Touch your leg.

B: (Touches her foot.)

A: Please try again.

B: (Touches her leg.)

A: You've got it!

If they do it right, you can say:	If they do not do it right, you can say:
Yes! **Nice work!**	**Please try again!**
Good! **You're right!**	
Great! **You've got it!**	
Good job!	

11.14 When can you come in?

> I'd like to make an appointment.
> How about _____?
> When can you come in?
> When would you like to come in?

Read these conversations with your teacher.

Dialogue ❶

At the dentist . . .

A: Hello, Dr. Chou's office.

B: Yes, I'd like to make an appointment for a checkup.

A: Okay, when can you come in?

B: How about next Thursday at 10:00 a.m.?

A: I'm sorry, she already has an appointment at 10:00. How about 11:00 a.m.?

B: That's fine.

A: What's your name?

B: Vera Lenin.

A: Okay Vera, we'll see you next Thursday at 11:00 a.m.

B: Thank you.

A: You're welcome. Bye.

B: Bye-bye.

Dialogue ❷

At the hair salon . . .

A: Hello, Salon Simone. May I help you?

B: Yes, I'd like to make an appointment with Brian.

A: Okay, when would you like to come in?

B: How about next Friday at 2:00 p.m.?

A: Oh, I'm sorry, he already has an appointment at 2:00. How about 3:00?

B: That's fine.

A: What's your name?

B: Jen Gomez.

A: Okay, Jen. We'll see you next Friday at 3:00 p.m.

B: Thank you.

A: You're welcome. Bye-bye.

B: Bye.

Dialogue ❸

RECEPTIONIST: Doctor's office. May I help you?

PATIENT: Yes, this is _____. I'm not feeling well. I'd like to make an appointment to see the doctor.

RECEPTIONIST: What's wrong?

PATIENT: I have _____. /My _____ hurts.

RECEPTIONIST: When can you come in?

PATIENT: How about _____ at _____?

RECEPTIONIST: That's fine. See you then.

PATIENT: Thank you. Goodbye.

11.15 How about Wednesday at 3:00?

Partner A

Take turns making appointments with your partner.

You are the caller first. Remember to fill in your calendar. Make appointments with your:

1. doctor
2. teacher
3. dentist
4. hairstylist

When you are the receptionist, don't forget to fill in your calendar. Answer the telephone:

1. Hello, doctor's office. May I help you?
2. Hello, this is Mrs. Stevens. How can I help you?
3. Good morning, Dr. Cotter's office.
4. Good afternoon, Hair Care. Can I help you?

	Monday	Tuesday	Wednesday	Thursday	Friday
9:00	Breakfast with Ann				
10:00			Meeting with Scott		
11:00					Meeting with Alan
Lunch					
1:00				Meeting with Patty	
2:00	English Class		English Class		English Class
3:00			Tennis with Eve		

11.15 How about Wednesday at 3:00?

Partner B

Take turns making appointments with your partner.

You are the receptionist first. Remember to fill in your calendar. Answer the telephone:

1. Hello, doctor's office. May I help you?
2. Hello, this is Mrs. Stevens. How can I help you?
3. Good morning, Dr. Cotter's office.
4. Good afternoon, Hair Care. Can I help you?

When you are the caller, don't forget to fill in your calendar. Make appointments with your:

1. doctor
2. teacher
3. dentist
4. hairstylist

	Monday	Tuesday	Wednesday	Thursday	Friday
9:00		English Class	Swimming	English Class	
10:00		English Class		English Class	
11:00	Meeting with Alex				
Lunch					
1:00					
2:00		Meeting with Cathy			
3:00					Meeting with Book Club

11.16 What do you do?

My name is Jim Cutter. I'm a barber. I work in a barbershop. I cut men's hair. Sometimes fathers bring their sons in for a haircut. I work from Monday to Saturday. I'm off on Sunday.

My wife is a hairstylist. She works in a hair salon. She cuts and styles hair for men and women. She works from Tuesday to Saturday. She has Sunday and Monday off.

1. What does Jim do?   _____

2. Where does he work?   _____

3. What does his wife do?   _____

4. Where does she work?   _____

Use these words to complete the sentences.

dentist   receptionist   pediatrician   nurse   doctor

1. I am a _____. I work in a doctor's office. I answer the telephone.

2. I am a _____. I am a doctor for children.

3. I am a _____. I work in a clinic. I help sick people.

4. I am a _____. I help people keep their teeth healthy.

5. I am a _____. I work in a hospital. I help the doctor.

Where do these people work? What do they do? Write the answers.

1. a hairstylist   _____

                         _____

2. a barber   _____

                         _____

3. a dental assistant   _____

                         _____

11.17 Guide to Staying Healthy

Keys to Good Health

- Get plenty of rest.
- Exercise regularly.
- Eat lots of fruit and vegetables.
- Don't eat too much fat or sugar.
- Get regular checkups with your doctor.
- Get your children immunized on time.

Keeping Your Teeth Healthy

- Brush your teeth three times a day.
- Floss once a day.
- See your dentist twice a year.
- Don't eat too many sweets.

Healthy Living Checklist

Do you . . .	YES	NO
get plenty of exercise?	☐	☐
eat plenty of fruit and vegetables?	☐	☐
eat lots of fatty foods?	☐	☐
eat foods with a lot of sugar?	☐	☐
get regular checkups?	☐	☐
brush your teeth three times a day?	☐	☐
floss once a day?	☐	☐
see your dentist twice a year?	☐	☐

How is your health?

great   **good**   **fair**   **poor**

11.18 How often do you . . .?

A: Kim, how often do you eat fruit?

B: Three times a day.

A: How often do you eat vegetables?

B: Three times a day.

A: How often do you exercise?

B: Twice a week.

A: How often do you see your dentist?

B: Twice a year.

0	never	a day
1x	once	a week
2x	twice	a month
3x	three times	a year
4x	four times	

Ask your classmates.

Name	Eat Fruit	Eat Vegetables	Exercise	See the Dentist

11.19 Writing About Someone's Health

Write about one of your classmates and how he or she stays healthy.

_____

_____

_____

_____

_____

_____

_____

What Do You Like to Do?

12.1 Vocabulary Presentation

12.2 Speaking

PARTNER **A:** *Look at page 151.*

PARTNER **B:** *Look at page 152. Say the words.*

PARTNER **A:** *Point to the picture.*

Change roles and repeat.

It's summer.

It's fall/autumn.

It's winter.

It's spring.

It's sunny.

It's cloudy.

It's hot.

It's cold.

It's raining.

It's snowing.

It's windy.

It's foggy.

12.3 Writing

Listen to your teacher. Write the words.

1. _____   3. _____   5. _____

2. _____   4. _____   6. _____

12.4 Partner to Partner

Say a word to your partner. Listen and write.

1. _____   3. _____   5. _____

2. _____   4. _____   6. _____

12.5 What's today's weather?

What's today's weather?	_____
What season is it?	_____

Answer the questions.

Yes, I do

No, I don't.

1. Do you need an umbrella today?   _____

2. Do you need sunglasses today?   _____

3. Do you need a jacket today?   _____

4. Do you need a raincoat today?   _____

5. Do you need gloves today?   _____

12.6 What kind of weather do you like?

Do you like . . .?   Yes, I do.   No, I don't.

Ask your classmates. Write yes or no.

Name	Rain	Snow	Fog	Hot Weather	Cold Weather

12.7 What's the weather in Canada and the U.S.?

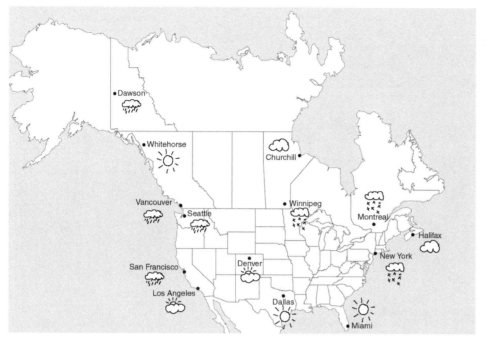

Look at the weather map for Canada and the U.S. Answer the questions T *(true) or* F *(false).*

1. It's sunny in San Francisco.   _____

2. It's cloudy in Miami.   _____

3. It's partly cloudy in Los Angeles.   _____

4. It's sunny in New York City.   _____

5. It's raining in Vancouver.   _____

6. It's raining in Whitehorse.   _____

7. It's snowing in Dawson.   _____

8. It's sunny in Dallas.   _____

12.8 Write about the weather.

Use the map above to answer these questions.

1. What's the weather in San Francisco?   _____

2. What's the weather in Montreal?   _____

3. What's the weather in Seattle?   _____

4. What's the weather in Halifax?   _____

5. What's the weather in Winnipeg?   _____

6. What's the weather in Denver?   _____

12.9 What's the weather in . . .?

Partner A

Look at the map. Tell your partner about the weather in Asia.

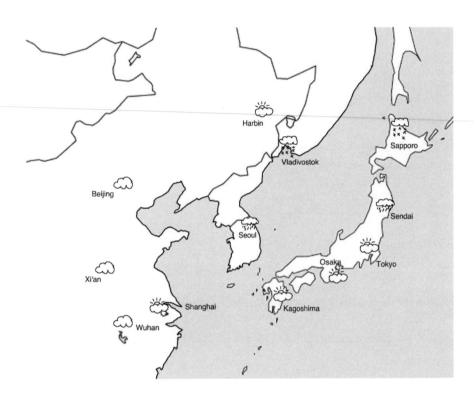

Ask your partner about the weather in Africa and the Middle East. Ask about these cities.
Write the answers.

What's the weather in _____?   *It's _____.*

1. Cairo   _____

2. Kuwait City   _____

3. Dakar   _____

4. Lagos   _____

5. Nairobi   _____

6. Kinshasa   _____

7. Pretoria   _____

8. Cape Town   _____

12.9 What's the weather in . . .?

Partner B

Look at the map. Tell your partner about the weather in Africa and the Middle East.

Ask your partner about the weather in Asia. Ask about these cities. Write the answers.

What's the weather in _____?   **It's** _____.

1. Tokyo _____

2. Beijing _____

3. Osaka _____

4. Seoul _____

5. Shanghai _____

6. Vladivostock _____

7. Sapporo _____

8. Kagoshima _____

12.10 **What's the weather in your hometown?**

A: David, where are you from?

B: I'm from Taipei, Taiwan.

A: What's the weather like there now?

B: It's hot and humid.

Ask your classmates about the weather in their hometowns.

Name	Hometown	Weather

hot	snowy	sunny
warm	rainy	cloudy
cool	foggy	humid
cold	windy	dry

12.11 Sports and Recreation

Write the word under the picture.

Play	volleyball	basketball	baseball	football
	soccer	ping-pong/table tennis	hockey	tennis

_____   _____   _____   _____

_____   _____   _____   _____

Go	bowling	cycling/biking	swimming	skating
	surfing	fishing	hiking	camping

_____   _____   _____   _____

_____   _____   _____   _____

12.12 What kind of sports do you like?

A: What sports do you like to play?

B: I like to play basketball.

A: What kind of sports do you like to watch?

B: I like to watch soccer.

Ask your classmates.

Name	Play	Watch

Challenge: Can you name the four balls?

_____   _____   _____   _____

12.13 Favorite Sports

Look at the information about your classmates above. Write about five of your classmates.

_____

_____

_____

_____

_____

12.14 What's on TV?

	7:30	8:00	8:30	9:00	9:30
Channel 2	Seinfeld	American Idol		24	
Channel 4	Entertainment Tonight	Dr. Phil		Will & Grace	Just Shoot Me
Channel 5	Hollywood Squares	World Cup Soccer			
Channel 7	Monday Night Football			Movie: Shrek	
Channel 9	Wall Street Report	Antiques Road Show	Washington Week	Before Stonewall	

Look at the TV listings. Answer the questions.

1. Which channels have sports programs? _____

2. What time can you watch soccer? _____

3. On which channel? _____

4. How many movies are on? _____

5. How many half-hour programs are on this schedule? _____

6. How long is *American Idol*? _____

12.15 Contact Assignment

Check your local TV listings.

1. What are the local TV channels in your area?

_____

2. Find three things that you want to watch. Write the channel, the date, the time, and the name of the program.

_____

_____

_____

12.16 What did you watch on TV last night?

What did you watch on TV last night?

What channel was it on?

What time was it on?

Ask your classmates.

Name	Program	Channel	Time

12.17 Find someone who . . .

Ask your classmates, **"Do you like . . .?"** *If they answer "Yes," write their name.*

1. _____ likes to play soccer.

2. _____ likes to go camping.

3. _____ likes to play basketball.

4. _____ likes to play football.

5. _____ likes to play volleyball.

6. _____ likes to play tennis.

7. _____ likes to go fishing.

8. _____ likes to go swimming.

9. _____ likes to go cycling.

10. _____ likes to go bowling.

11. _____ likes hot weather.

12. _____ likes rain.

13. _____ likes fog.

14. _____ likes snow.

15. _____ likes winter.

16. _____ likes spring.

17. _____ likes fall.

18. _____ likes to watch baseball.

19. _____ likes to watch football.

20. _____ likes to watch soccer.

12.18 In My Free Time

Reading 1

My name is Nancy. My favorite season is summer. I love water sports. I usually swim three times a week, and I go water skiing once or twice a year. I also like hiking, tennis, and cycling. I don't like playing team sports. On sunny weekends I like to go to the beach for a picnic and a long walk. I love being outside, so I don't like watching TV.

Writing

Answer the questions.

1. What is Nancy's favorite season? _____

2. What water sports does Nancy like? _____

3. Does Nancy like playing team sports? _____

4. What does Nancy like to do when the weather is sunny? _____

Reading 2

My name's Bob. I'm a high school student. I love playing team sports. In the fall, I play football and soccer on school teams. During the winter, I play ice hockey with my friends on a pond near our neighborhood. In the spring, I play baseball and volleyball on city teams, and I play tennis with my brother once a week. In the summer, I usually go swimming, fishing, and surfing on the weekends. During the week, I work to earn enough money so that I can pay for all my recreational activities!

Writing

Answer the questions.

1. What does Bob do? _____

2. What team sports does Bob play in the fall? _____

3. Where does Bob play ice hockey in the winter? _____

4. Who does Bob usually play tennis with? _____

5. What water sports does Bob like? _____

6. What does Bob do during the week? _____

Answer the questions about yourself.

1. What is your favorite season? _____

2. What do you like to do in your favorite season? _____

3. What are your favorite sports? _____

4. What other activities do you like? _____

12.19 What I Like to Do

Write about what you like to do in your free time. What do you do in each season?
What sports do you like to watch? What sports do you like to play?

_____

_____

_____

_____

_____

_____

_____

_____

_____

_____

_____

_____

_____

12.20 What are you going to do this weekend?

A: What are you going to do this weekend?

B: I'm going to play soccer on Saturday. What about you?

A: I'm going to do laundry.

Walk around and find out what your classmates are going to do this weekend.

1. _____

_____

2. _____

_____

3. _____

_____

4. _____

_____

5. _____

_____

6. _____

_____

7. _____

_____

12.21 What's your favorite season?

What's your favorite season?

What's your favorite kind of weather?

What are your favorite sports?

Ask your classmates.

Name	Favorite Season	Favorite Weather	Favorite Sports

12.22 Contact Assignment

Look at a newspaper or watch the news. Write about the weather for tomorrow and the next day.

_____

_____

_____

_____

_____

_____

_____

UNIT 13

How Do You Get to School?

13.1 Vocabulary Presentation

①

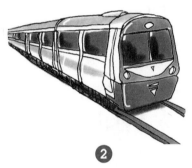
②

③

④

⑤

⑥

⑦

LAKELAND BUS CO.

Bus Pass
Admit One

Valid Dates:
June 2004—2005

3211-006-004-79ada

⑧

CITYLINE BUS COMPANY

BUS TRANSFER
SEPT 29 2004
12:01 PM.---
1371021 008 5211

⑨

13.2 Speaking

PARTNER A: *Look at page 169.*

PARTNER B: *Look at page 170. Say the words.*

PARTNER A: *Point to the picture.*

Change roles and repeat.

bus

train

subway

car

motorcycle

bicycle/bike

bus stop

bus pass

transfer

13.3 Writing

Listen to your teacher. Write the words.

1. _____   3. _____   5. _____

2. _____   4. _____   6. _____

13.4 Partner to Partner

Say a word to your partner. Listen and write.

1. _____   3. _____   5. _____

2. _____   4. _____   6. _____

13.5 Does this bus go to the post office?

Partner A

Find out where the bus goes. Ask your partner, "Does this bus go to _____?"

> **the post office**
>
> **the bank**
>
> **Appleby's Supermarket**
>
> **Cliff's Hardware Store**
>
> **Wash and Dry Laundromat**
>
> **Heartland Drugstore**

Your partner will look at his/her map and answer.

Write down the names of the places where the bus goes.

_____   _____

_____   _____

Answer your partner's questions.

> **Yes, it does.**
>
> **No, it doesn't.**

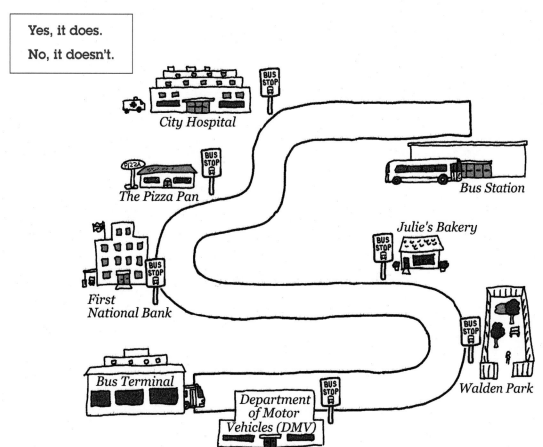

13.5 Does this bus go to the post office?

Partner B

Answer your partner's questions.

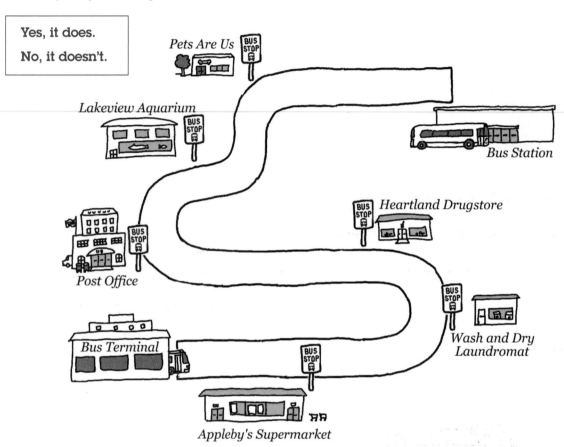

| Yes, it does. |
| No, it doesn't. |

Find out where the bus goes. Ask your partner, **"Does this bus go to _____?"**

the bank

Julie's Bakery

the mall

the Department of Motor Vehicles (DMV)

City Hospital

Nick's Department Store

Your partner will look at his/her map and answer.

Write down the names of the places where the bus goes.

_____   _____

_____   _____

13.6 How do you get to school?

by bicycle/bike	by subway
by bus	by train
by car	by taxi
by motorcycle	on foot

I get to school _____.   *I go to work* _____.

Ask your classmates.

How do you get to school?

How do you go to work?

Name	School	Work

13.7 How do we get to school?

Write about yourself. How do you get to school? How do you go to work?

_____

_____

Write about your classmates.

Max comes to school on foot. He goes to work by bus.

1. _____

2. _____

3. _____

4. _____

5. _____

13.8 How long does it take?

A: How long does it take to get to school?
B: It takes 5 minutes on foot.
A: How long does it take to get to work?
B: It takes 45 minutes by bus.

Walk around and ask your classmates.

How long does it take to get to school?

How long does it take to get to work?

It takes . . .

Name	School	Work

13.9 Reading a Map

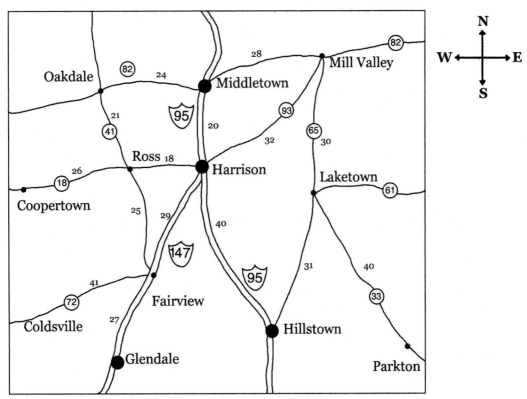

Look at the map. Answer the questions.

1. What highway do you take to get from Middletown to Hillstown? _____

2. What direction do you go to get from Middletown to Hillstown? _____

3. How many miles is it from Middletown to Hillstown? _____

4. How many miles is it from Hillstown to Middletown and back? _____

Look at the map and ask your partner questions.

How do I get from _____ **to** _____?

How many miles is it from _____ **to** _____?

What direction do I go to get from _____ **to** _____?

13.10 Getting to Work

Reading 1

Greta, Colby, and Ben work in the same office. Greta takes the bus to work every day. It takes her 15 minutes. Colby walks to the bus station. He takes the bus downtown and then transfers to the subway. It takes him 50 minutes. Ben usually rides his bicycle to work when it's not raining. When it's raining, he drives his car. He prefers to ride his bike because it's much cheaper, and he likes the exercise. It takes him 40 minutes to get to work by bike but 20 minutes to get to work by car.

Writing

Answer the questions.

1. How does Greta get to work?   _____

2. How long does it take Colby to get to work?   _____

3. How long does it take Ben to get to work?   _____

Reading 2

Claudia is late for work today because the bus was late. Claudia's boss is worried because Claudia has a lot of work to do. Claudia says, "I'm sorry, the bus was late." Her boss says, "It's okay. I understand." She asks Claudia, "Can you work late today?" Claudia says, "Yes, I can. Today I have no plans." Claudia's boss thanks her, and they both go back to work.

Writing

Answer the questions.

1. Why is Claudia late for work?   _____

2. Why is Claudia's boss worried?   _____

3. What does Claudia's boss ask her?   _____

4. Why does Claudia agree to work late?   _____

13.11 Were you . . .?

Yes, I was.

No, I wasn't.

1. Were you hungry this morning? _____

2. Were you late for class today? _____

3. Were you busy this morning? _____

4. Were you tired yesterday? _____

5. Were you happy last weekend? _____

6. Were you sick last week? _____

I He She It	was
You We They	were

13.12 Find someone who . . .

Ask your classmates, **"Do you . . .?"** *If they answer "Yes," write their name.*

1. _____ takes the bus to school.

2. _____ comes to school by car.

3. _____ has a bicycle.

4. _____ likes motorcycles.

5. _____ has a driver's license.

6. _____ has a bus pass.

7. _____ takes the subway.

8. _____ has a car.

9. _____ likes to walk.

10. _____ studies English on the bus.

11. _____ lives near a bus stop.

12. _____ takes the bus to work.

13. _____ sometimes takes the subway.

14. _____ walks to school.

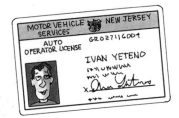

13.13 Reading a Bus Schedule

42 University/North Gate

NORTHBOUND				SOUTHBOUND			
Univ.	Ashby Lane	Center Street	North Gate	North Gate	Center Street	Ashby Lane	Univ.
5:40 AM	5:45	5:53	6:03	6:20	6:30	6:39	6:44
6:10	6:15	6:23	6:33	6:50	7:00	7:09	7:14
6:40	6:45	6:53	7:03	7:20	7:30	7:39	7:44
7:10	7:15	7:23	7:33	7:50	8:00	8:09	8:14
7:40	7:45	7:53	8:03	8:20	8:30	8:39	8:44
8:10	8:15	8:23	8:33	8:50	9:00	9:09	9:14
8:40	8:45	8:53	9:03	9:20	9:30	9:39	9:44
9:10	9:15	9:23	9:33	9:50	10:00	10:09	10:14

Look at the bus schedule. Answer the questions.

1. What is the bus number? _____

2. What is the name of the bus route? _____

3. Where does this bus go? _____, _____, _____,

   _____

4. What time does the first bus leave the university? _____

5. How long does it take to get from the university to North Gate? _____

Write the missing names of the bus stops.

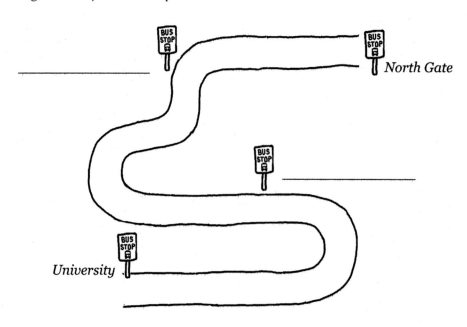

13.14 Reading a Town Map

Look at the map. Write the names of these places in the correct place.

1. The *coffee shop* is next to the movie theater.
2. The *bank* is across the street from the coffee shop.
3. The *East Wind Restaurant* is on the corner of Elm Street and Green Street.
4. The *supermarket* is next to Tom's Bowling Alley.
5. The *laundromat* is between The Pizza Place and the Palace Drugstore.

Movie Theater		History Museum	Apartment Building		Jefferson High School

Black Road

| Internet Café | | Midtown Park | | Tom's Bowling Alley | |
| Post Office | | | | | Auto Shop |

Oak St.   Elm St.

Green Street

| Hardware Store | | Palace Drugstore | The Pizza Place | Central Library | General Hospital |

13.15 Asking for Directions

Write the words under the pictures.

turn right	turn left	go straight (ahead)

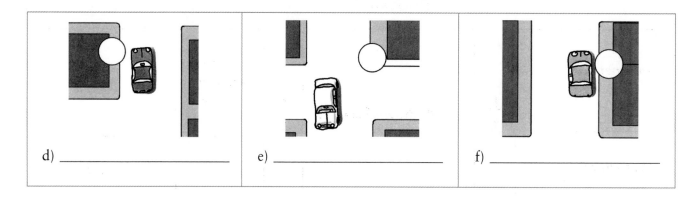

a) _____

b) _____

c) _____

on the right	on the left	on the corner

d) _____

e) _____

f) _____

at the end of the street	go past	on the corner of _____ and _____

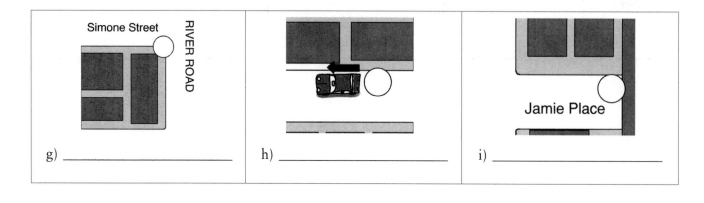

g) _____

h) _____

i) _____

13.16 Listening to Directions

Look at the map. Listen to your teacher. Write the number on the map.

13.17 How do I get to . . .?

A: Excuse me, how do I get to *the bank?*

B: Go straight to the first corner and turn right. Go straight. It's on the left next to the hardware store.

A: Thank you.

Partner A

Ask your partner how to get to these places. Follow your partner's directions. Find each place on the map. Write the place on the map.

1. the department store   2. the coffee shop   3. the museum   4. the hospital

Tell your partner how to get to these places.

1. the drugstore   2. the library   3. the gas station   4. the high school

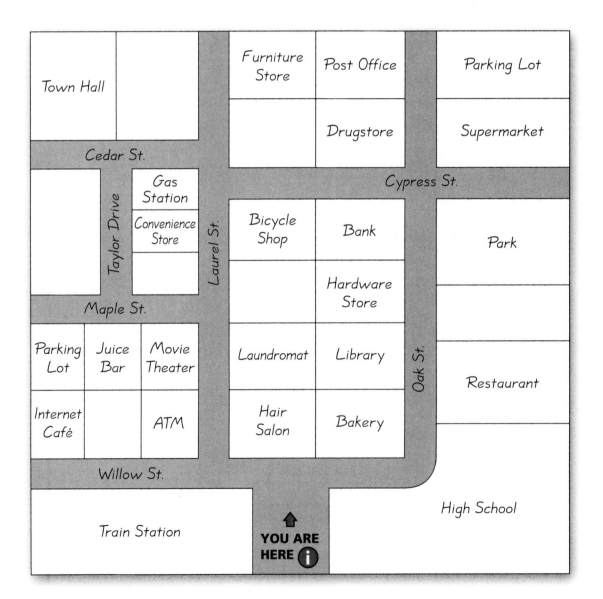

13.17 How do I get to . . .?

A: Excuse me, how do I get to *the bank?*

B: Go straight to the first corner and turn right. Go straight. It's on the left next to the hardware store.

A: Thank you.

Partner B

Tell your partner how to get to these places.

1. the department store   2. the coffee shop   3. the museum   4. the hospital

Ask your partner how to get to these places. Follow your partner's directions. Find each place on the map. Write the place on the map.

1. the drugstore   2. the library   3. the gas station   4. the high school

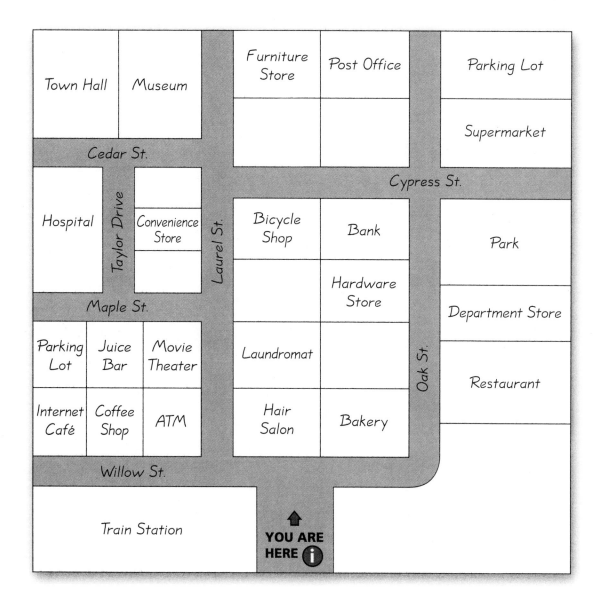

13.18 Where do you go?

Write about your daily life. Where do you go? How do you get there?

_____

_____

_____

_____

_____

_____

13.19 Transportation Signs and Symbols

Work with a partner. Match the symbols with the meanings.

_____ 1. pedestrian crossing

_____ 2. no left turn

_____ 3. hard hat area

_____ 4. railroad crossing

_____ 5. people working

_____ 6. falling rocks

_____ 7. one-way

_____ 8. gas

_____ 9. do not enter

_____ 10. telephone

13.20 Contact Assignments

Bring in a bus, train, or subway schedule or a road map of your area. Talk with a partner.
Write down three ideas or questions.

_____

_____

_____

_____

_____

_____

When you are outside, look for these signs. See how many you can find.

1.

2.

3.

4.

5.

6.

7.

8.

9.

10.